Compilation of Water-Resources Data and Hydrogeologic Setting for the Allison Woods Research Station in Iredell County, North Carolina, 2005–2008

By Brad A. Huffman and Joju Abraham

Prepared in cooperation with the North Carolina Department of Environment and Natural Resources, Division of Water Quality

Open-File Report 2010–1015

U.S. Department of the Interior
U.S. Geological Survey

U.S. Department of the Interior
KEN SALAZAR, Secretary

U.S. Geological Survey
Marcia K. McNutt, Director

U.S. Geological Survey, Reston, Virginia: 2010

For more information on the USGS—the Federal source for science about the Earth, its natural and living resources, natural hazards, and the environment, visit http://www.usgs.gov or call 1-888-ASK-USGS

For an overview of USGS information products, including maps, imagery, and publications, visit http://www.usgs.gov/pubprod

To order this and other USGS information products, visit http://store.usgs.gov

Suggested citation:
Huffman, B.A., and Abraham, Joju, 2010, Compilation of water-resources data and hydrogeologic setting for the Allison Woods research station in Iredell County, North Carolina, 2005–2008: U.S. Geological Survey Open-File Report 2010–1015, 56 p.

Contents

Figures

Tables

Conversion Factors

Inch/Pound to SI

Multiply	By	To obtain
Length		
inch (in.)	2.54	centimeter (cm)
foot (ft)	0.3048	meter (m)
mile (mi)	1.609	kilometer (km)
Area		
acre	0.4047	hectare (ha)
square mile (mi^2)	2.590	square kilometer (km^2)
Volume		
gallon (gal)	3.785	liter (L)
Flow		
gallon per minute (gal/min)	0.06309	liter per second (L/s)
million gallons per day (Mgal/d)	0.04381	cubic meter per second (m^3/s)
Pressure		
pound per square inch (lb/in^2)	6.895	Kilopascal (kPa)
Radioactivity		
picocurie per liter (pCi/L)	0.037	becquerel per liter (Bq/L)

Temperature in degrees Celsius (°C) may be converted to degrees Fahrenheit (°F) as follows:

$$°F = (1.8 \times °C) + 32$$

Vertical coordinate information is referenced to the North American Vertical Datum of 1988 (NAVD 88).

Water-quality measurements used in this report:

µS/cm   microsiemens per centimeter at 25 degrees Celsius
µg/L   microgram per liter
mg/L   milligram per liter

Compilation of Water-Resources Data and Hydrogeologic Setting for the Allison Woods Research Station in the Piedmont Physiographic Province of North Carolina, 2005-2008

By Brad A. Huffman[1] and Joju Abraham[2]

Abstract

Water-resources data were collected to describe the hydrologic conditions at the Allison Woods research station near Statesville, North Carolina, in the Piedmont Physiographic Province of North Carolina. Data collected by the U.S. Geological Survey and the North Carolina Department of Environment and Natural Resources, Division of Water Quality, from April 2005 through September 2008 are presented in this report.

Data presented include well-construction characteristics and periodic groundwater-level measurements for 29 wells, borehole geophysical logs for 8 wells, hourly groundwater-level measurements for 5 wells, continuous water-quality measurements for 3 wells, periodic water-quality samples for 12 wells and 1 surface-water station, slug-test results for 11 wells, and shallow groundwater-flow maps. In addition, the geology and hydrogeology at the site are summarized.

Introduction

In 1999, the U.S. Geological Survey (USGS) and the North Carolina Department of Environment and Natural Resources (NCDENR), Division of Water Quality (DWQ), began a multiyear cooperative study to measure the ambient groundwater quality and describe the groundwater-flow systems at selected research stations in the Piedmont and Blue Ridge Physiographic Provinces of North Carolina (Daniel and Dahlen, 2002). The study is supported by the Piedmont and Mountains Resource Evaluation Program (PMREP), which was initiated by the North Carolina Legislature to ensure the long-term availability, sustainability, and quality of groundwater in the State. The study was designed to be a 10-year, intensive field investigation at research stations established in representative hydrogeologic settings across the State. To date (2008), 12 research stations have been selected for study in the Piedmont and Blue Ridge Physiographic Provinces (fig. 1), and wells have been installed at 10 of these research stations.

One of the primary objectives of the PMREP in installing research stations in representative hydrogeologic settings is to evaluate the spatial and temporal variation of ambient groundwater levels and groundwater-quality data across the Piedmont and Blue Ridge Physiographic Provinces. The research stations generally consist of topographic transects of monitoring-well clusters located parallel to an assumed flow path within a conceptual "slope-aquifer" system, described by LeGrand and Nelson (2004), from recharge to discharge areas. Well clusters are designed to monitor separate zones in the groundwater system, including the shallow regolith, transition zone, and deep bedrock (Chapman and others, 2005). These zones characterize the conceptual components of the Piedmont and Mountains groundwater system (Harned and Daniel, 1992; fig. 2). Data from the research stations provide information to refine the historical conceptual groundwater-flow models for the Piedmont and Blue Ridge Physiographic Provinces in North Carolina and the Southeastern United States.

The Allison Woods research station (AWRS) was established to determine the hydrogeologic characteristics of the regolith-bedrock aquifer system in the North Carolina piedmont. The AWRS was selected to represent a mafic gneiss hydrogeologic unit in the Inner Piedmont litho-tectonic terrane (fig. 3). The primary objectives of this study are to evaluate the effects of (1) the mafic gneiss rock type and shallow dipping foliation, (2) thickness and composition of the regolith, (3) thickness and characteristics of the transition zone, and (4) the development and characteristics of bedrock fractures on groundwater flow and quality. The study conducted at the AWRS was designed to (a) distinguish and evaluate groundwater in the three zones—the shallow regolith, transition zone, and the deep bedrock, and (b) evaluate the conceptual slope-aquifer system (LeGrand and Nelson, 2004) of the Piedmont and Mountains groundwater system. Thus, the components of the groundwater system at AWRS are characterized in relation to hydrogeologic properties and water quality.

---

[1] U.S. Geological Survey.

[2] North Carolina Department of Environment and Natural Resources, Division of Water Quality.

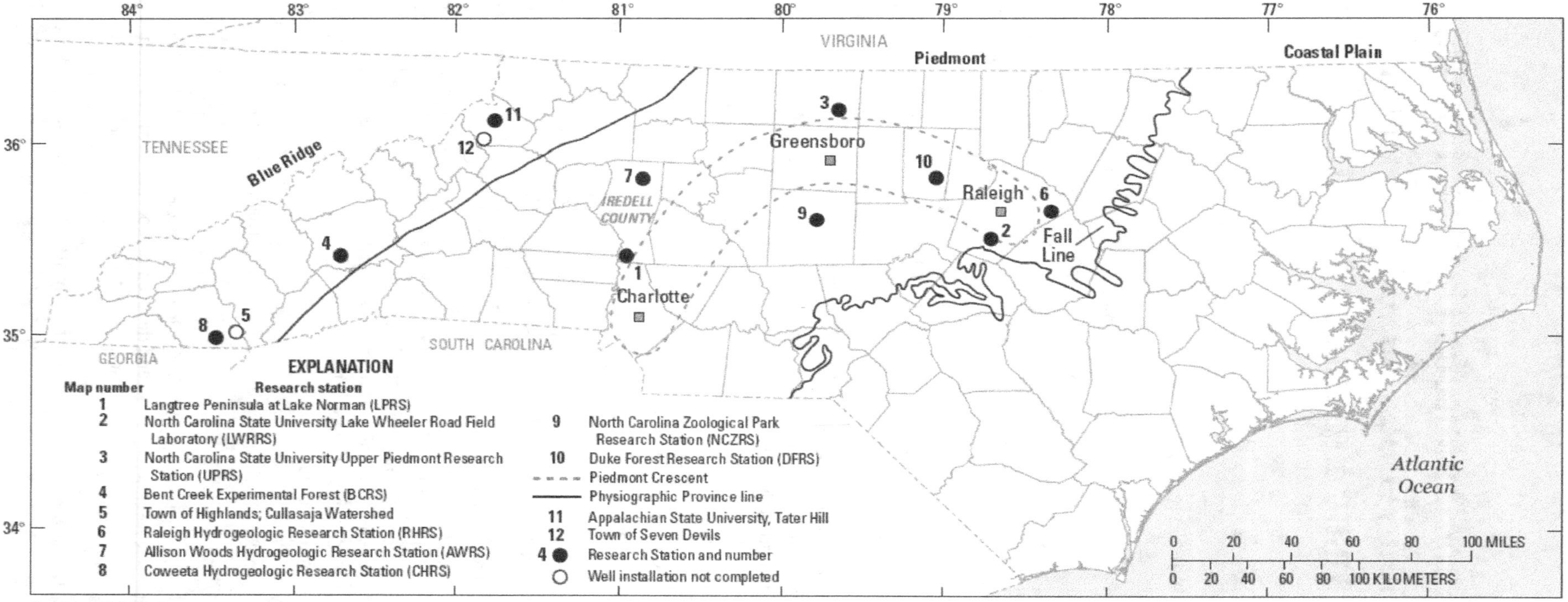
84°
83°
82°
81°
80°
79°
78°
77°
76°
36°
35°
34°
VIRGINIA
Piedmont
Coastal Plain
TENNESSEE
Blue Ridge
GEORGIA
SOUTH CAROLINA
Greensboro
Raleigh
Charlotte
IREDELL COUNTY
Fall Line
Atlantic Ocean
0 20 40 60 80 100 MILES
0 20 40 60 80 100 KILOMETERS
EXPLANATION
Map number
Research station
1 Langtree Peninsula at Lake Norman (LPRS)
2 North Carolina State University Lake Wheeler Road Field Laboratory (LWRRS)
3 North Carolina State University Upper Piedmont Research Station (UPRS)
4 Bent Creek Experimental Forest (BCRS)
5 Town of Highlands; Cullasaja Watershed
6 Raleigh Hydrogeologic Research Station (RHRS)
7 Allison Woods Hydrogeologic Research Station (AWRS)
8 Coweeta Hydrogeologic Research Station (CHRS)
9 North Carolina Zoological Park Research Station (NCZRS)
10 Duke Forest Research Station (DFRS)
Piedmont Crescent
Physiographic Province line
11 Appalachian State University, Tater Hill
12 Town of Seven Devils
4 Research Station and number
Well installation not completed

Base from digital files of:
U.S. Department of Commerce, Bureau of Census,
1990 Precensus TIGER/Line Files-Political boundaries, 1991
U.S. Environmental Protection Agency, River File 3
U.S. Geological Survey, 1:100,000 scale

Figure 1 Locations of research stations selected for investigations as part of the cooperative U.S Geological Survey and North Carolina Department of Environment and Natural Resources, Division of Water Quality, Piedmont and Mountains Resource Evaluation Program in North Carolina.

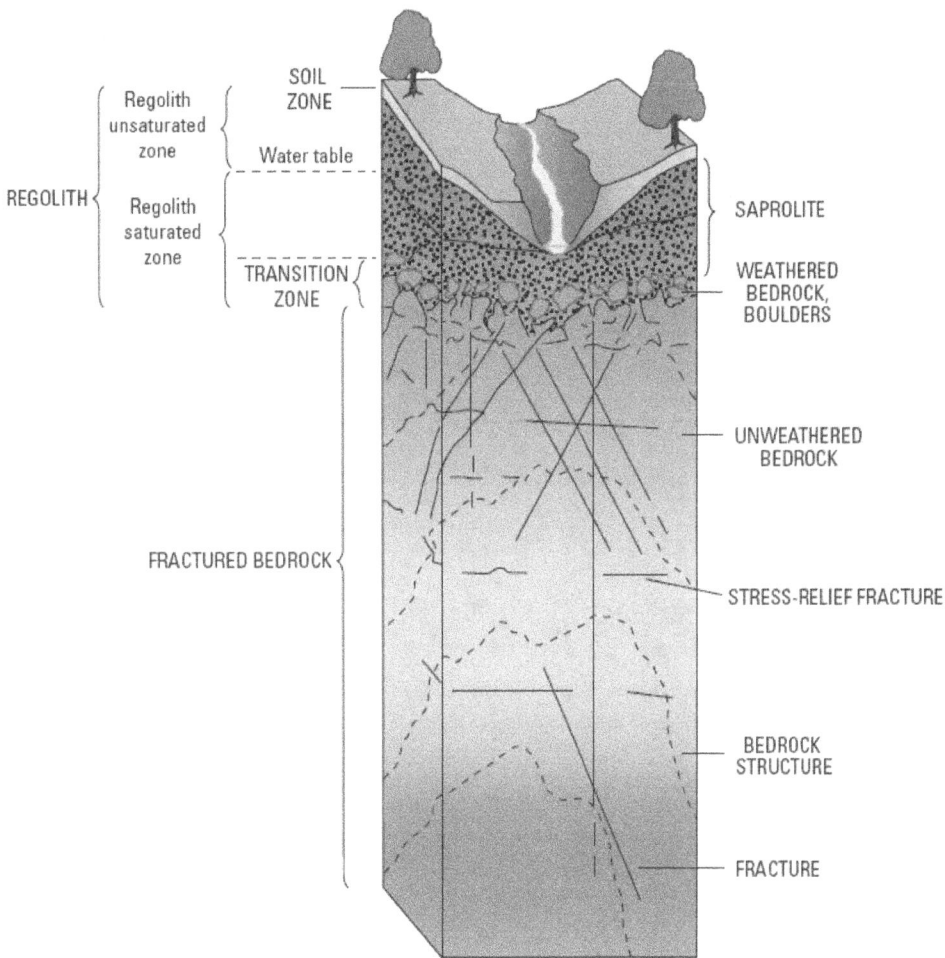

Figure 2.   Conceptual components of the groundwater system in the North Carolina Piedmont and Mountains (from Harned and Daniel, 1992).

Background

The Piedmont and Blue Ridge Physiographic Provinces in North Carolina encompass about 30,544 square miles (mi²) in 65 counties (fig. 1). Groundwater is the primary source of drinking water in most rural and some suburban areas of the State, whereas surface water is the primary drinking-water source in the metropolitan areas (Daniel and Dahlen, 2002). Most of the population lives in or near the metropolitan areas of Raleigh/Durham/Chapel Hill, Greensboro/Winston-Salem, and Charlotte, all of which are located in the Piedmont Physiographic Province (Chapman and others, 2005) in an area known as the "Piedmont Crescent" (fig. 1). In 2005, the population of this area was about 6.7 million, and about one-third of the population used groundwater as their primary water supply. Total groundwater use was estimated to be about 248 million gallons per day (Mgal/d; U.S. Geological Survey, 2008b).

The geology of most of the Piedmont and Blue Ridge Provinces is complex. Rocks have undergone several episodes of intense metamorphism, folding, faulting, and igneous intrusion. In North Carolina, the regional sequences of rocks are grouped into belts (North Carolina Geological Survey, 1985; fig. 3A). Although the rocks within a given belt generally are similar with respect to lithology, more variation and complexity can be observed on a local scale. Daniel and Dahlen (2002) provided an overview of the major hydrogeologic units of the Piedmont and Blue Ridge Provinces with reference to the geologic belts of the State.

Groundwater in the Piedmont and Blue Ridge Physiographic Provinces occurs in complex hydrogeologic settings composed of assemblages of metamorphic, igneous, and sedimentary rocks and secondary fracture networks. Weathered regolith, which is composed of soil, saprolite, alluvium, and colluvium, overlies the fractured bedrock (fig. 2) and provides storage to the underlying fractures in the bedrock (Heath, 1980). Groundwater flows through intragranular pore spaces or through relict fractures in soil and saprolite. In contrast, groundwater in the underlying bedrock flows through secondary fractures and discontinuities because the unweathered bedrock has very low primary porosity and permeability.

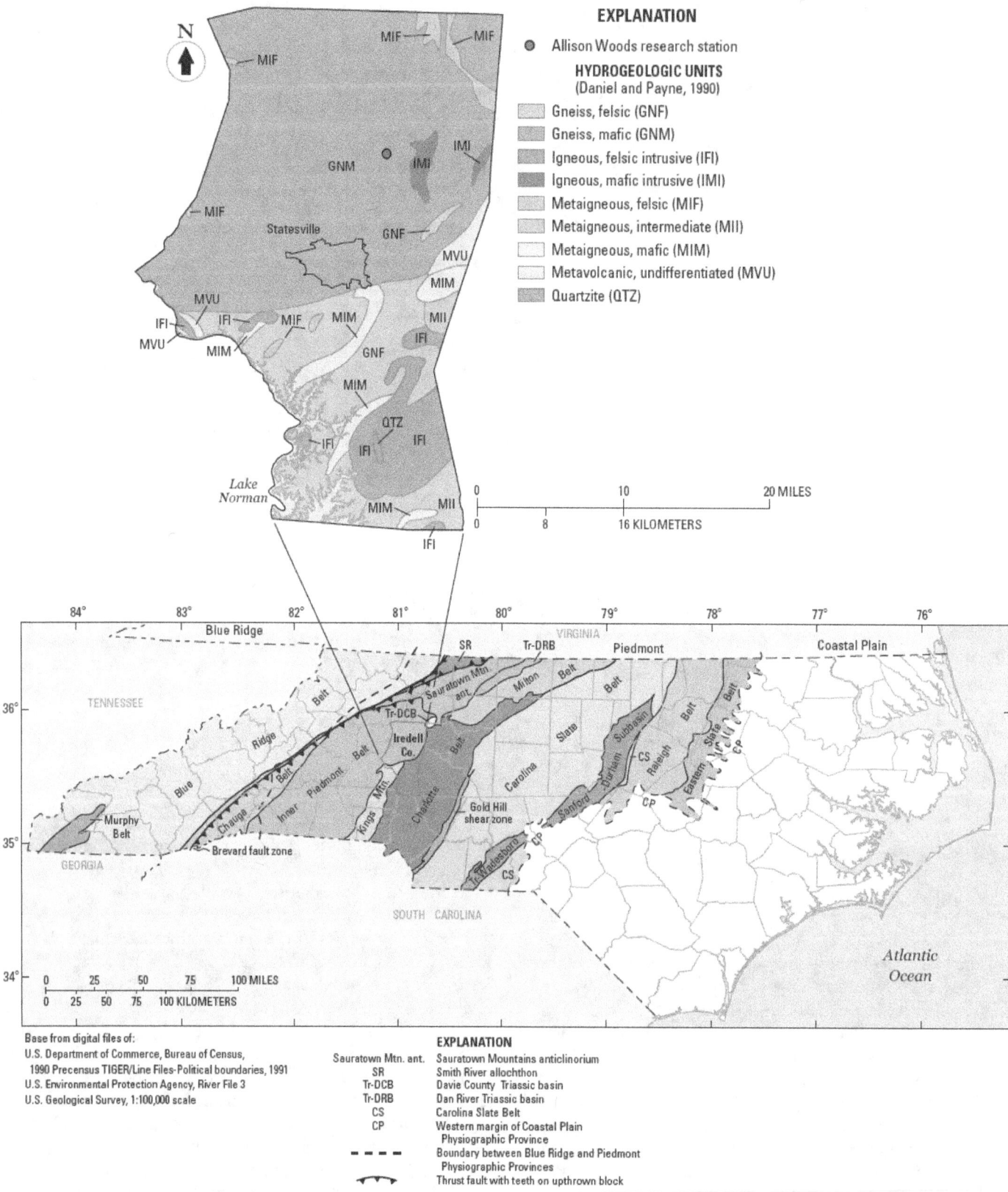

Figure 3A. Locations of Allison Woods research station, hydrogeologic units in Iredell County, and geologic belts delineated in North Carolina (modified from North Carolina Geological Survey, 1985; Daniel and Payne, 1990).

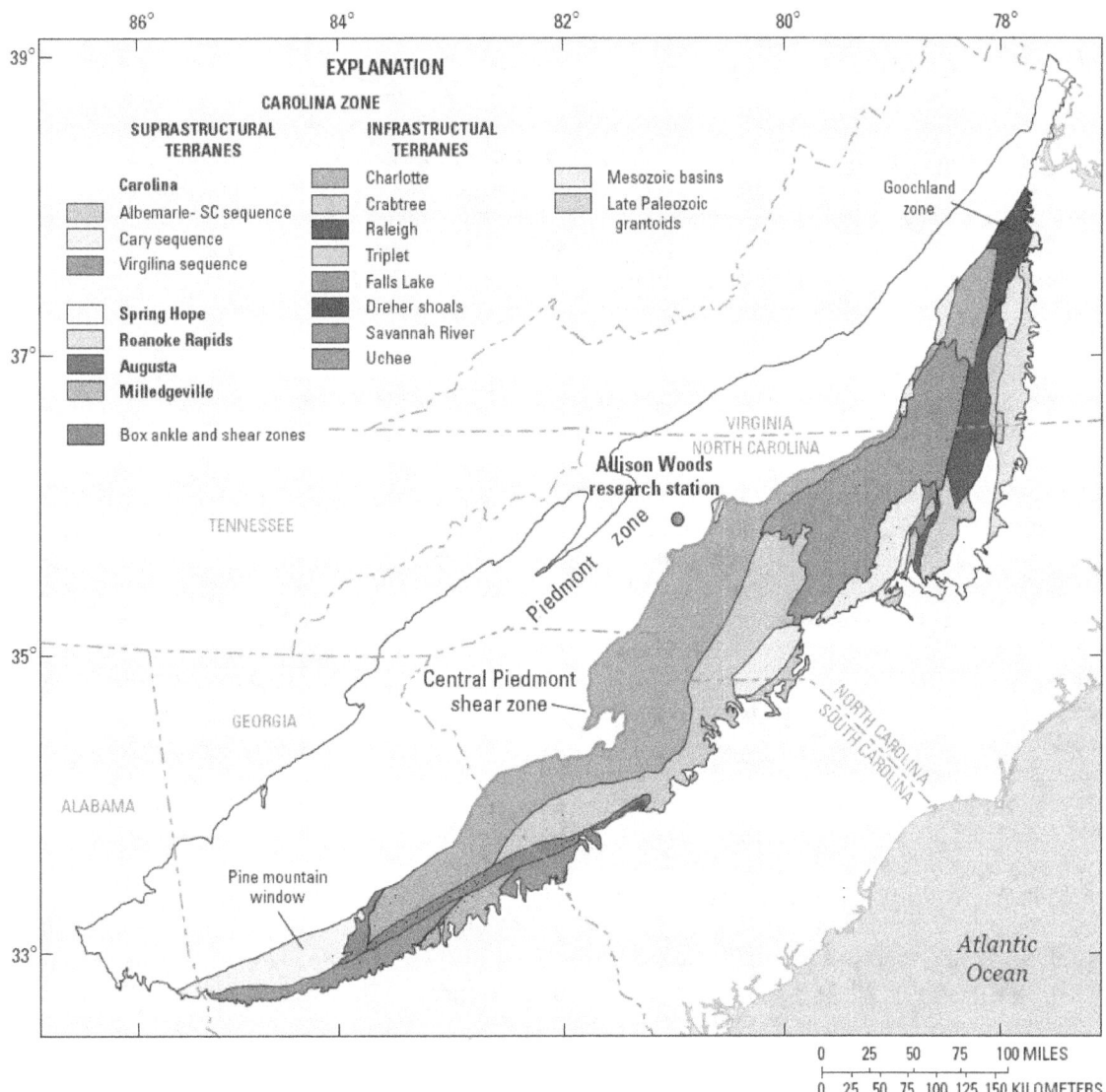

Figure 3B.   Geologic map of structured terranes in the Piedmont of Georgia, South Carolina, North Carolina, and Virginia (adapted from Hibbard and others, 2002).

Piedmont aquifers, though simply described as a two-component (regolith and bedrock) groundwater system, commonly have a third component—the transition zone, which provides the hydraulic connection between the regolith and bedrock through numerous open fractures. Conceptual models for groundwater flow in the Piedmont and Mountains groundwater systems have been described by Daniel and Dahlen (2002) and LeGrand and Nelson (2004). Typically, natural groundwater recharge occurs in uplands and along slopes, while groundwater discharge occurs in valleys.

Description of the Study Area

The AWRS is the sixth hydrogeologic research station installed as part of the PMREP (fig. 1). The study area encompasses approximately 25 acres, about 10 miles northeast of the center of Statesville in Iredell County, North Carolina (fig. 3A). The latitude and longitude of the approximate center of the site is 35° 54′ 28.52″ N. and 80° 49′ 30.30″ W. The AWRS is located on the Allison Woods Foundation property and partially on the William Locke Allison, Jr., Forest Preserve, which is part of the Allison Woods Foundation property (fig. 4). The Allison Woods Foundation was created in 1991 to conserve the natural, historical, and cultural attributes of Allison Woods and William Locke Allison, Jr., Forest Preserve. An unnamed tributary flowing along the western edge of the property empties into another unnamed perennial stream, eventually joining Rocky Creek, which is a major tributary of the South Yadkin River (fig. 4).

The humid, subtropical climate in the study area is typical for the Southeastern United States. The State Climate Office of North Carolina maintains a meteorological data station (Turnersburg 318778; State Climate Office of North Carolina, 2008) located about 1 mile south of the AWRS (fig. 4). On the basis of precipitation records for the period 1998 to 2007, the average annual precipitation for the 10-year period is estimated to be 41 inches. Hydrologic conditions during water years[1] 2007–08 were affected by drought conditions (U.S. Geological Survey, 2007). Annual precipitation for these years (through September 2008) was 31 and 33 inches, respectively.

The AWRS represents a rural setting where residents rely primarily on groundwater from private wells in the bedrock zone as the main source of potable water. The site has been managed as forestland in recent decades, but intensive crop cultivation may have existed historically as indicated by extensively eroded areas near the stream. The topography at the site gently slopes from the hilltop to the bottom slope. The altitude difference between the hilltop and the stream bottom is about 80 ft (fig. 5).

Tectonically, the AWRS is located in the Inner Piedmont litho-tectonic terrane (fig. 3A). Based on the geologic map of Goldsmith and others (1988), rocks at the AWRS are metamorphosed to amphibolite grade, consisting of biotite gneiss

and amphibolite with subordinate mica schist. The biotite gneiss and amphibolite (CZbga) unit is described as interlayered biotite gneiss, hornblende gneiss, amphibolite, metagabro, and subordinate mica schist (Goldsmith and others, 1988). Limited exposures of rocks along the streambed at the AWRS indicate shallow-dipping rocks consisting of biotite gneiss, amphibolite, and kyanite schist.

The surficial geology at the AWRS is composed of metamorphic rocks ranging in composition from biotite gneiss, amphibolite to amphibolite gneiss, and biotite-garnet-kyanite schist to kyanite schist, as indicated by boulders, floats, and limited outcrops observed near the stream. Floats represented by quartzite and vein quartz are also present but to a lesser extent. Limited outcrop exposures indicate that the rocks strike approximately east-west and dip about 20° to the north. The biotite gneiss is fine- to medium-grained and consists of quartz, plagioclase, biotite, hornblende, and lesser amounts of garnet, epidote, and iron oxides. The amphibolite schist is fine- to medium-grained and contains variable amounts of hornblende and biotite. Both biotite gneiss and amphibolite (hornblende) schist are present generally as floats on the hilltop and mid-slope areas. Kyanite schist is characterized by the presence of kyanite blades and biotite with variable amounts of garnet and generally is observed on the mid-slope and bottom-slope areas at the site.

According to the hydrogeologic map by Daniel and Payne (1990), the AWRS is located in the mafic gneiss (GNM) hydrogeologic unit, which represents about 18 percent of the Piedmont and Blue Ridge Provinces in North Carolina (Daniel and Dahlen, 2002). The mafic gneiss unit is described as a dark gray to green to black, fine- to coarse-grained biotite hornblende gneiss. It commonly exhibits distinct layering and foliation, and is often interbedded with biotite and hornblende gneisses and schists, and occasional amphibolite layers (Daniel and Dahlen, 2002). Based on well yields from several thousand wells, wells drilled into the mafic gneiss have an average yield of about 20 gallons per minute (gal/min), and the GNM hydrogeologic unit is ranked fifth among the 18 hydrogeologic units described by Daniel and Dahlen (2002).

Purpose and Scope

The purpose of this report is to summarize data collected from April 2005 through September 2008 at the AWRS. Investigative activities at the AWRS included the collection and logging of 4 soil and rock cores totaling 475 feet (ft), installation of 16 observation wells (including coreholes) grouped into 4 clusters aligned along topographic transects (A–A′, B–B′, fig. 4), installation of 13 piezometers for water-level and aquifer-test monitoring, installation of a real-time DCP for continuous monitoring of water levels and water quality in all 3 wells at well cluster MW-2 (fig. 5), monthly collection of water levels, semiannual sampling of wells and an unnamed tributary (USGS station 02117495), a 24-hour aquifer test (not presented in this report), slug tests, and borehole geophysical logs.

---

[1] Water year is the period from October 1 through September 30 and is identified by the year in which the period ends. The 2008 water year, for example, was the period October 1, 2007, through September 30, 2008.

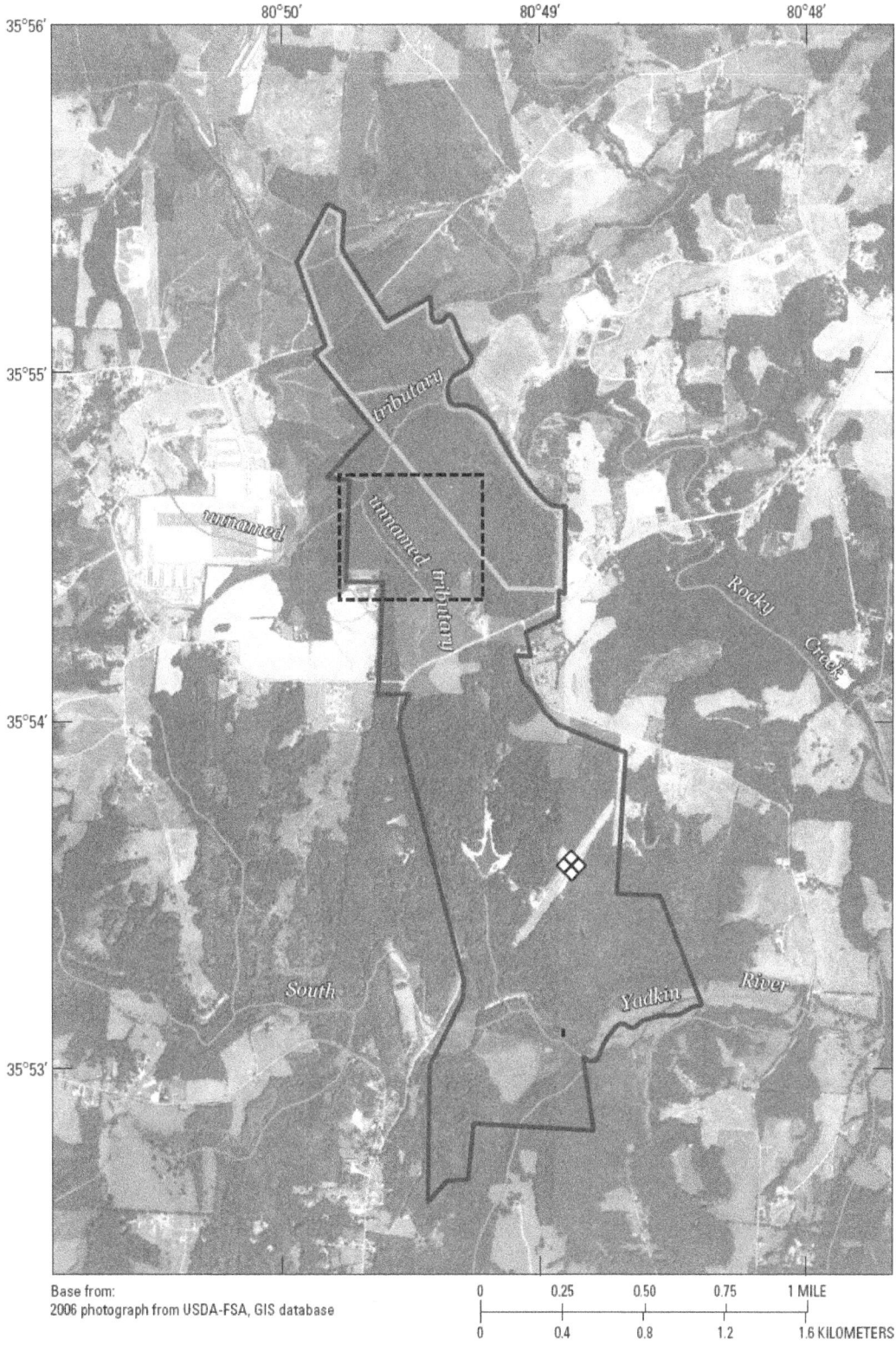

0   0.25   0.50   0.75   1 MILE

0   0.4   0.8   1.2   1.6 KILOMETERS

EXPLANATION

- - - - -   Approximate site boundary

━━━━━   Allison Woods Foundation property

━━━━━   William Locke Allison, Jr., Forest Preserve of
the Allison Woods Foundation property

◈   Climate station

Figure 4. Aerial photograph showing Allison Woods Foundation property, approximate location of research station, and climate station.

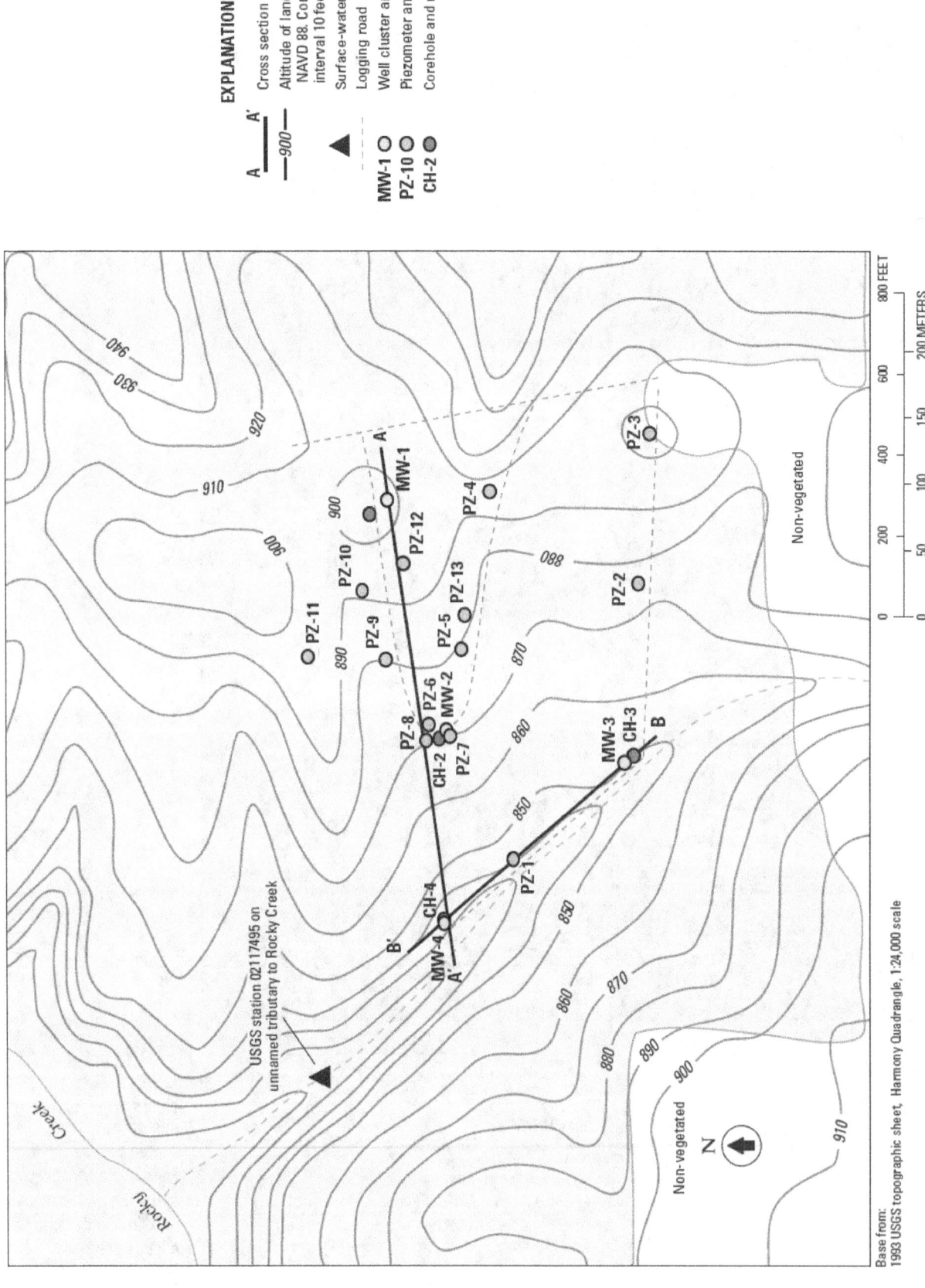

Base from:
1993 USGS topographic sheet, Harmony Quadrangle, 1:24,000 scale

Figure 5.   Topographic features, locations of well clusters, and lines of section at the Allison Woods research station in Iredell County, North Carolina.

Methods of Data Collection

Geologic Coring

Continuous soil and bedrock cores were collected at each monitoring well cluster location. The cores provide a continuous profile of soil to bedrock at each well cluster, which were used to determine the construction requirements for the monitoring wells.

Methods for conducting the geologic coring are described in Chapman and others (2005) and NCDENR DWQ's Standard Operating Procedures for the Resource Evaluation Program (*http://h2o.enr.state.nc.us/gwp/documents/GWREP_SOP-Draft_Apr_08.pdf*; accessed August 2009). The coreholes were drilled by using a wire-line coring rig owned and operated by the NCDENR DWQ. A 5-ft-long, 2.5-inch inside diameter core barrel sampler was used with a wire-line retrieval system. A carbide-tipped sampling core barrel bit was used to penetrate the unconsolidated material, and a diamond-tipped bit was used to penetrate the competent bedrock. Detailed descriptions of the regolith and bedrock cores are included in the appendices of this report.

Each well cluster, consisting of a shallow well, a transition-zone well, and a deep well, is designed to monitor three separate zones in the groundwater system—the regolith, the transition zone between regolith and bedrock, and the deeper bedrock. Thirteen piezometers were also installed at the site to conduct aquifer tests and to describe the horizontal and vertical groundwater flow.

Shallow Regolith and Transition Zone Wells

The shallow and transition-zone regolith wells were drilled using air rotary methods. After the boring reached the prescribed depth, a 4-inch PVC well casing was placed in the boring. All the shallow and transition-zone wells were constructed with 0.01-inch well screens that ranged in length from 10 to 20 ft. Clean sand filter material was used to fill the annular space between the PVC casing and the borehole to 2 ft above the top of the well screen, except for transition-zone wells located on the ridge top (MW–1I) and mid-slope (MW–2I), in which sand was filled to 9 to 20 ft above the top of the well screen. Bentonite was placed above the sand filter to 3 ft below land surface. The top 3 ft of the annular space was grouted with cement.

Bedrock Wells

A 12-inch air hammer was used to set the surface casings for all the bedrock monitoring wells. Bedrock casing borings were terminated after about 5 ft of competent bedrock was penetrated. A 6-inch diameter PVC casing was used to support the regolith material. The annular space between the PVC and the borehole was filled with rock cuttings and native material up to 20 ft below land surface, except for the well located on the ridge top, which was filled to 47 ft below land surface. Above the rock cuttings, bentonite filled the annular space to 3 ft below land surface. The top 3 ft of the annular space was grouted with cement. A smaller (6-1/4-inch diameter) drill bit was used to drill the open borehole section of the bedrock to depths up to 400 ft.

Piezometers

Thirteen piezometers were installed in the regolith to depths ranging from 14 to 39 ft by using a hydraulic probe. The piezometers were drilled to the top of the transition zone. Each piezometer was constructed with a 1-inch diameter PVC casing and a 0.1-inch slotted screen. A filter pack consisting of fine sand was placed to at least 2 ft above the well screen and topped with bentonite.

Coreholes

A 4-inch steel surface casing was used in all the coreholes. Bentonite was placed in the annular space from the bedrock to up to 3 ft below land surface, and the top 3 ft was cemented. The remainder of the corehole was completed as an open borehole. The coreholes were also used to monitor water level and water quality.

Well and Surface-Water Numbering System

The well and surface-water numbering system is described in Chapman and others (2005). The well descriptors used in this study are as follows: MW for monitoring well, CH for corehole, and PZ for piezometer. Following the well descriptor is a cluster number and a letter, which indicates the aquifer section or zone that is being monitored: S for shallow zone (regolith), I for transition zone, and D for deeper zone (bedrock). For example, well MW–1S is a monitoring well in cluster 1 and is completed in the shallow regolith zone.

Borehole Geophysical Logging

Borehole geophysical logs were collected in two phases. The first phase of geophysical logging included the collection of traditional logs—caliper, natural gamma, electrical (resistance, short-normal, long-normal, and lateral resistivity), and fluid (temperature, fluid resistivity) logs. The second phase of logging included the collection of a borehole image by using an oriented digital camera, the optical televiewer (OTV). The OTV data enable the identification of lithology type (felsic or mafic), rock-foliation orientation, and fracture orientation. The orientation data are displayed in tadpole plots, where dip angle is plotted as a circle and azimuth direction is plotted as a line segment. The OTV data were corrected for magnetic declination and borehole deviation (azimuth and inclination angle). All geophysical logs collected and reported here are referenced to feet below land surface (Chapman and others, 2005).

Continuous Monitoring

Continuous monitoring of water levels and water quality was conducted at five wells at the AWRS. Data were collected at hourly intervals. Data from the three wells in well cluster MW-2 included water levels and water-quality parameters that were recorded on a data-collection platform (DCP) and transmitted by satellite every 4 hours to the USGS National Water Information System (NWIS) database for processing and then made accessible from the USGS North Carolina Water Science Center Web page at *http://nc.water.usgs.gov.* Continuous water-level data for wells MW-1D and MW-4D were periodically downloaded and manually entered in the USGS NWIS database.

Groundwater levels were measured by using a submersible pressure transducer that had an internal datalogger. The pressure transducers were checked periodically against a steel or electric tape to ensure accurate readings. Water-level data are stored in the NWIS database relative to feet below land surface. In this report, groundwater-level data are presented in feet above the North American Vertical Datum of 1988 (NAVD 88). Groundwater-level data collected at the AWRS during water years 2007–08 are published in USGS annual data reports (U.S. Geological Survey, 2008a, 2009).

Continuous groundwater-quality stations were established in three wells (MW-2 cluster). Water-quality parameters were measured by using multiparameter water-quality probes, and data were recorded using the DCP. Methods for collecting continuous water-quality data are described in Huffman and others (2006).

Periodic Water-Level Measurements

Periodic groundwater levels were measured monthly at all of the wells at the AWRS to identify seasonal groundwater trends in each of the three zones (regolith, transition zone, and fractured bedrock) and to evaluate vertical hydraulic gradients between wells in each cluster. Methods for collecting periodic water-level measurements are described in Huffman and others (2006). Water-level data were entered into the USGS Ground Water Site Inventory (GWSI) part of the NWIS database and are available online at *http://nwis.waterdata. usgs.gov/nc/nwis/gwlevels,* and in USGS annual data reports (U.S. Geological Survey, 2008a, 2009). In this report, periodic groundwater levels are presented in feet above NAVD 88.

Slug Tests

Rising and falling slug tests were performed on 11 of the monitoring wells to assess the hydraulic conductivity across the AWRS. Methods used for collecting slug-test data are described in Huffman and others (2006). The slug-test data for this investigation were analyzed using the Bouwer and Rice (1976) method within the spreadsheets developed by Halford and Kuniansky (2002).

Aquifer Test

A 24-hour constant rate aquifer test was conducted during October 22–23, 2007, to observe the response of fracture networks and overlying regolith to pumping stress. A variable-speed, 4-inch diameter submersible pump was installed in well MW-2D at a depth of 197 ft. The pump was supported by 1.25-inch diameter PVC pipe, and a 1.5-inch diameter polyethylene hose was used to discharge water approximately 200 ft north of the pumped well. A digital, in-line flowmeter was used to determine discharge rates, and the flow rates were verified manually with a graduated 5-gallon bucket and stopwatch. The following wells and piezometers were instrumented with electronic pressure transducers to monitor water levels: MW-1I, MW-1D, MW-2S, MW-2I, MW-2D, CH-2, MW-3D, MW-4D, CH-4, PZ-6, PZ-7, and PZ-9. The remaining wells and piezometers were measured manually at regular intervals throughout the aquifer test. Based on a step-drawdown test conducted on October 16, 2007, an optimum pumping rate of 18 gal/min was maintained for the aquifer test.

Water-Quality Sampling and Laboratory Analysis

Water-quality samples were collected from each monitoring well (except dry wells), selected coreholes, and a nearby stream at the AWRS by following standard USGS protocols (Wilde and others, 1999). Samples were collected at the site by the USGS during two sampling events in November 2006 and July 2007. Sampling methods for collecting water-quality data are described in Huffman and others (2006). Analytical results of the water-quality sampling for November 2006 and July 2007 are presented in this report and published in the USGS annual data report (U.S. Geological Survey, 2008a).

Water samples were analyzed by the USGS National Water Quality Laboratory in Denver, Colorado. The water-quality constituents analyzed by the USGS laboratory included major ions, nutrients, metals, and radon 222 (gas). Of these, samples for major ions and nutrients were collected during each sampling event.

The NCDENR DWQ conducted additional water-quality sampling at the site. The analytical results for the DWQ water-quality samples are not presented in this report, but are available online at *http://h2o.enr.state.nc.us/gwp/Summary_ AllisonWoods.htm* (accessed August 2009). Water-quality constituents analyzed by the DWQ laboratories included major ions, nutrients, trace metals, and selected organic chemicals.

Statistical Analysis of Water-Quality Data

Box plots, Piper (1953) diagrams, and Stiff (1951) diagrams were used to analyze the statistical and geochemical variability in the periodic water-quality data. Methods used for the statistical analyses of water-quality data are described in Huffman and others (2006).

In this report, water-quality data are presented by surface water and by groundwater-system zone (regolith, transition zone, and bedrock) for those samples analyzed by the USGS laboratory. DWQ laboratory results are not used in the statistical analyses presented in this report.

Allison Woods Research Station

Well Construction

Four groundwater monitoring-well clusters, each consisting of 3 wells and 1 corehole, were constructed along with 13 piezometers at the AWRS (fig. 5). Construction methods were similar to those described in Chapman and others (2005). Well cluster locations were selected to provide water-quality and water-level data along a topographic transect encompassing areas of recharge and discharge based on conceptual models developed for the slope-aquifer system (LeGrand and Nelson, 2004). Criteria for well locations included topographic position, accessibility, and site boundaries. Three well clusters are located along a topographic profile extending from hilltop to bottom-slope, corresponding to the recharge to discharge areas of the slope-aquifer system of LeGrand and Nelson (2004).

Well clusters MW-1 and MW-2 are located in a conceptual recharge areas, and well clusters MW-3 and MW-4 are located in conceptual discharge areas near the unnamed tributary (USGS station 02117495). The 13 piezometers were installed in the shallow regolith to provide data during an aquifer test and to obtain detailed data to define the two-dimensional groundwater flow within the regolith. Well-construction information is provided in table 1.

Estimated bedrock well yields ranged from 10 to 30 gal/min, increasing from the hilltop to the bottom-slope wells; MW-3D is an exception with a yield of only 2 gal/min. Increased yields (up to 20 gal/min) were also noted in the transition-zone wells located at the lower slope compared to the transition-zone wells in mid slope (1 gal/min) and hilltop (3 gal/min) areas.

Hydrogeologic Setting

The AWRS is located in the Inner Piedmont litho-tectonic belt and Piedmont zone (AWRS; figs. 3A, B) and is representative of the mafic gneiss (GNM) hydrogeologic unit. The geology at the AWRS is represented by shallow-dipping, low- to medium-grade metamorphic rocks consisting of kyanite-biotite schist, biotite gneiss, and amphibolite to amphibolite (hornblende) gneiss. The biotite gneiss and amphibolite gneiss are collectively described as interlayered biotite gneiss, hornblende gneiss, amphibolite, with subordinate mica schist and is comparable to the regional unit of CZbga of Goldsmith and others (1988). The kyanite-biotite schist contains kyanite, biotite, and garnet, with layers of quartz and feldspar bands. The rocks at the AWRS include considerable amounts of felsic minerals, represented by quartz and feldspars in the leucocratic zones.

Generalized hydrogeologic cross sections along two transects at the AWRS are shown in figure 6. Cross section A–A′ was constructed along the transect from well cluster MW-1 to well cluster MW-4 in a west-to-east direction. Cross section B–B′ was constructed along the transect from well cluster MW-3 to well cluster MW-4 in a south-to-north direction.

The depth to competent bedrock is approximately 70 ft in the upper-cluster cores (CH-1 and CH-2) and 30 to 40 ft in the lower-cluster cores (CH-3 and CH-4) (Appendixes 1A–1D). The generalized hydrogeologic profile along A–A′ (fig. 6A) indicates that the thickness of shallow regolith and transition zone is greater in the upper-cluster (hill-top and mid-slope) locations compared to the lower-cluster (bottom-slope) locations. Based on core lithology (Appendix 1), the transition zone generally is represented by schists, whereas the deeper bedrock is represented by biotite gneiss and amphibolite gneiss. The transition zone was almost indistinct in one of the lower cluster cores (CH-3). Well cluster MW-3 generally responded differently than the other well clusters.

The water-bearing fractures in the biotite gneiss dip mostly at low angles (<30°) in the biotite gneiss, but a fewer moderately dipping (30–60°) water-bearing fractures are also present. The water-bearing factures in the kyanite-biotite-schist predominantly dip at low angles, parallel to foliaton. Few water-bearing fractures exist in the amphibolite gneiss, which is generally observed in the bedrock zone near the stream.The groundwater system at the AWRS has two primary components: a shallow, weathered regolith and a deeper, unweathered bedrock. A transition zone consisting of partially weathered bedrock and saprolite generally is present between the regolith and bedrock in the three topographic settings at the site.

The regolith at the AWRS includes soil, residuum, and saprolite. The regolith is composed of reddish-brown, clayey silt with minor amounts of sand and mica, and becomes sandy silt with depth (Appendix 1). The saprolite generally consists of brown, yellowish-brown to olive-brown micaceous silt, displaying low-angle relict foliations, and grades into partially weathered rock.

The transition zone at the AWRS is characterized by partially weathered kyanite-biotite schists and numerous open low-angle fractures. The transition zone is recognized as the highly weathered zone near the top of bedrock that is fractured to a greater extent compared to the unweathered bedrock.

The bedrock fractures are characterized mostly by subhorizontal (<20°) to horizontal (20–40°) dip angles across the topographic profile. Moderate (40–60°) to (>80°) vertical-dipping fractures are fewer in number. The bedrock fractures showed evidence of water movement by the presence of FeO and MnO stains that decreased with depth. At least two major water-bearing fractures at each well location were identified along the cross-sectional profile A–A′ (fig. 6A) based on caliper and resistivity logs and well pumping. Drawdown observed during well sampling events (and during the 24-hour aquifer test) indicates a well-connected fracture system at the AWRS, particularly along the A–A′ topographic profile.

Table 1. Construction characteristics of monitoring wells at the Allison Woods research station, North Carolina.

[NAVD 88, North American Vertical Datum of 1988; MW, monitoring well; CH, corehole; S, shallow; PVC, polyvinyl chloride; R, regolith; I, transition zone; D, deep; B, bedrock; GS, galvanized steel; PZ, piezometer; na, not available]

Site identification	Station name (fig. 5)	Construction date	Land-surface altitude (feet above NAVD 88)	Casing material	Casing diameter (inches)	Screened interval or open borehole interval (feet below land surface) from	to	Screen type	Zone monitored
355429080492301	MW-1S	6/14/2005	899.42	PVC	4	20	35	0.01 slotted PVC	R
355429080492302	MW-1I	3/8/2006	899.11	PVC	4	55	70	0.01 slotted PVC	I
355429080492303	MW-1D	2/23/2006	898.96	GS	6.25	90	400	Open hole	B
355429080492304	CH-1	5/3/2005	899.71	GS	4	60	100	Open hole	I-B
355428080493001	MW-2S	6/14/2005	870.93	PVC	4	23	38	0.01 slotted PVC	R
355428080493002	MW-2I	10/18/2005	871.39	PVC	4	60	70	0.01 slotted PVC	I
355428080493003	MW-2D	10/4/2005	871.47	GS	6	87	400	Open hole	B
355428080493004	CH-2	4/7/2005	870.58	GS	4	60	200	Open hole	I-B
355422080493101	MW-3S	6/13/2005	851.05	PVC	4	7	16	0.01 slotted PVC	R
355422080493102	MW-3I	3/28/2006	849.46	PVC	4	25	35	0.01 slotted PVC	I
355422080493103	MW-3D	3/22/2006	849.05	GS	6.25	45	372	Open hole	B
355422080493104	CH-3	5/24/2005	851.02	GS	4	20	75	Open hole	I-B
355427080493701	MW-4S	6/8/2005	836.02	PVC	4	8	23	0.01 slotted PVC	R
355427080493702	MW-4I	3/15/2006	837.41	PVC	4	30	40	0.01 slotted PVC	I
355427080493703	MW-4D	3/9/2006	836.79	GS	6.25	45	300	Open hole	B
355427080493704	CH-4	5/24/2005	836.26	GS	4	33	100	Open hole	I-B
355426080493401	PZ-1	5/31/2005	843.38	PVC	1	9	14	0.01 slotted PVC	R
355422080492501	PZ-2	5/31/2005	871.76	PVC	1	19	24	0.01 slotted PVC	R
355422080492001	PZ-3	6/1/2005	895.35	PVC	1	23	37	0.01 slotted PVC	R
355426080492201	PZ-4	6/1/2005	888.61	PVC	1	33	38	0.01 slotted PVC	R
355427080492701	PZ-5	6/1/2005	880.27	PVC	1	32	37	0.01 slotted PVC	R
355428080493005	PZ-6	6/6/2005	872.19	PVC	1	30	35	0.01 slotted PVC	R
355427080493001	PZ-7	na	870.04	PVC	1	34	39	0.01 slotted PVC	R
355428080493006	PZ-8	na	871.33	PVC	1	24	29	0.01 slotted PVC	R
355429080492801	PZ-9	na	881.08	PVC	1	32	37	0.01 slotted PVC	R
355430080492501	PZ-10	6/7/2005	888.15	PVC	1	26	31	0.01 slotted PVC	R
355432080492801	PZ-11	na	894.70	PVC	1	28	33	0.01 slotted PVC	R
355429080492501	PZ-12	6/8/2005	895.47	PVC	1	34	39	0.01 slotted PVC	R
355427080492601	PZ-13	na	886.01	PVC	1	25	30	0.01 slotted PVC	R

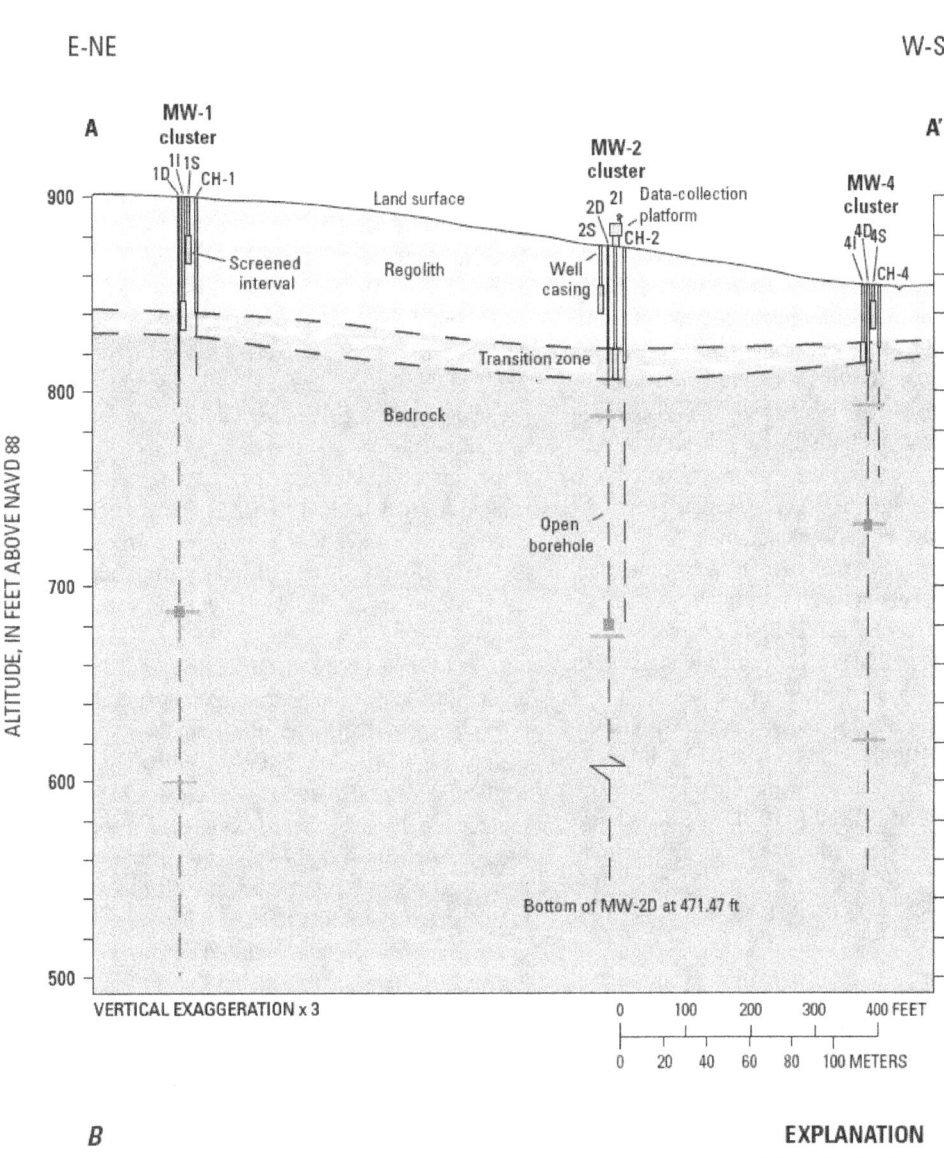

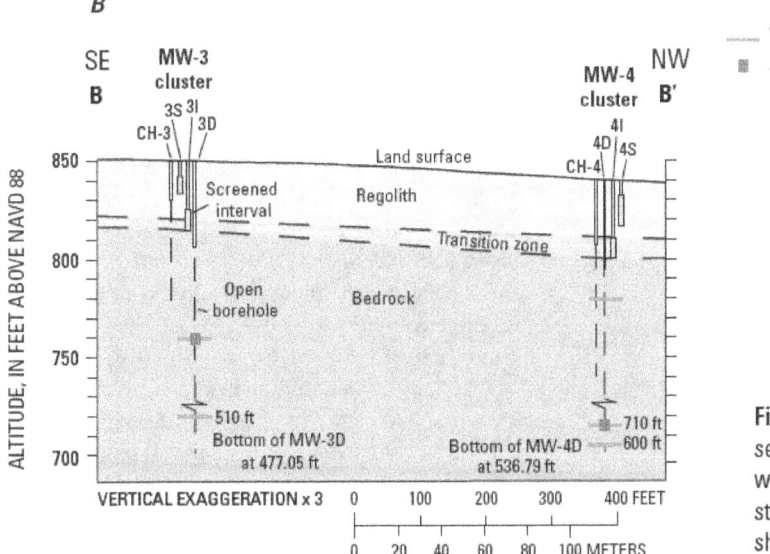

Figure 6. Generalized hydrogeologic cross sections *(A)* A–A′ and *(B)* B–B′ along the well transects at the Allison Woods research station, North Carolina (section locations are shown in figure 5).

Water-Resources Data

Borehole geophysical logs were collected from all four bedrock wells and all four coreholes at the AWRS (figs. 7–14). Data collected from these wells include caliper, natural gamma, short-normal and long-normal resistivity logs; fluid-temperature and fluid-resistivity logs; and OTV images (figs. 7–10). OTV images were not collected in the coreholes.

Slug tests were conducted in 11 wells at the AWRS in April 2007. A 5-ft long, 3.5-inch diameter PVC bailer was used to displace water in the wells. The purpose of the slug tests was to obtain estimates of hydraulic conductivity for the three aquifer zones tapped by the wells—the shallow regolith, transition zone, and bedrock. Results of slug-test analyses are provided in table 2. Because of slow recovery of MW-2I, slug-test data were not analyzed quantitatively for this well. Also, well MW-1S was dry when the slug tests were conducted.

A 24-hr constant-rate aquifer test was conducted to observe the response of fracture network and overlying regolith to pumping stress at the study site. Drawdown in the pumped well, MW-2D, was about 46 ft. In response to the pumping stress at MW-2D, corehole CH-2, located near the pumped well, and bedrock well MW-1D, located upslope to the pumped well (fig. 6), showed similar magnitude (43–44 ft) of drawdown and showed a similar drawdown pattern with time (fig. 15A). Bedrock well MW-4D and corehole CH-4, located downslope along the well transect A–A' (fig. 6), showed 5–6 ft of drawdown (fig. 15A). Bedrock well MW-3D, located along well transect B–B', showed a delayed response to the pumping and a drawdown of 1.6 ft. The 24 hours of pumping resulted in a slight measurable decline of 0.25 ft in a transition-zone well

(MW-2I, fig. 15B) that is located near the pumped well. Water levels in the shallow regolith wells and piezometers did not decline in response to the pumping stress (fig. 15B).

Monthly water levels were measured in all 29 wells (including piezometers) at the AWRS. Water levels have been measured in all wells since May 2006 (fig. 16). The period of record indicated on the figures in this report is from the initial month through September 2008. Wells MW-1S, PZ-3, and PZ-10 through PZ-13 were dry for the period of record. Groundwater altitudes at well cluster MW-1 ranged from about 853 to 858 ft in the transition zone (including CH-1) and about 829 to 834 ft in the bedrock zone. Groundwater altitudes at well cluster MW-2 ranged from about 841 to 847 ft in the shallow and transition zone and about 830 to 839 ft in the bedrock zone (including CH-2). Groundwater altitudes at well cluster MW-3 ranged from about 839 to 847 ft in all three zones. Groundwater altitudes at well cluster MW-4 ranged from about 824 to 828 ft in the shallow and transition zone and about 828 to 829 ft in the bedrock zone (including CH-4). The water-level altitudes for the bedrock zone were consistently lower than water-level altitudes in the shallow and transition zone at well clusters MW-1 and MW-2, indicating an area of recharge to the groundwater system. The water-level altitudes for the bedrock zone generally were higher than water-level altitudes in the shallow and transition zone at well clusters MW-3 and MW-4, indicating an area of ground-water discharge. However, well cluster MW-3 does not strictly represent a discharge area because the water-level altitude in the shallow well is higher than the altitude in the transition zone well (fig. 16C) Groundwater altitudes in the piezometers ranged from about 831 to 856 ft. Detailed summaries of groundwater-level data recorded in the AWRS wells for water years 2007–08 are published in USGS annual data reports for North Carolina (U.S. Geological Survey, 2008a, 2009).

Continuous groundwater levels have been recorded hourly in three wells in cluster MW-2 since January 2008 (fig. 17). Continuous groundwater levels also have been recorded every 15 minutes in bedrock wells MW-1D and MW-4D. These groundwater levels are plotted from January 2008 to July 2008 (fig. 18). There are no data for wells MW-1D and MW-2D from May 27 to May 30, or for MW-4D from May 27 to June 30, because of the removal of the pressure transducer used to monitor water levels during these periods.

Groundwater altitude maps were constructed for two water-level extremes for the AWRS during the period May 2006 to September 2008. Near maximum and minimum water levels measured in the shallow regolith wells and a grid of piezometers were used to construct these groundwater altitude maps for the shallow regolith (fig. 19).

A total of five sampling events were conducted between November 2006 and May 2008 at the AWRS. Results from all five sampling events were analyzed by the NCDENR's DWQ laboratory and are provided in an Excel® spread-sheet and published on the Internet at *http://h2o.enr.state. nc.us/gwp/Summary_AllisonWoods.htm* (accessed online in August 2009).

Table 2. Analytical results of slug tests in wells at the Allison Woods research station, North Carolina.

Well number	Screened/open interval (feet below land surface)	Hydraulic conductivity (feet per day)
Regolith wells		
MW-2S	23–38	1.0
MW-3S	7–16	3.0
MW-4S	8–23	3.0
Transition-zone wells		
MW-1I	55–70	1.0
MW-2I	60–70	<0.1*
MW-3I	25–35	2.0
MW-4I	30–40	7.0
Bedrock wells		
MW-1D	90–400	0.2
MW-2D	87–400	0.7
MW-3D	45–372	0.1
MW-4D	45–300	1.0

* Recovery too slow to quantify.

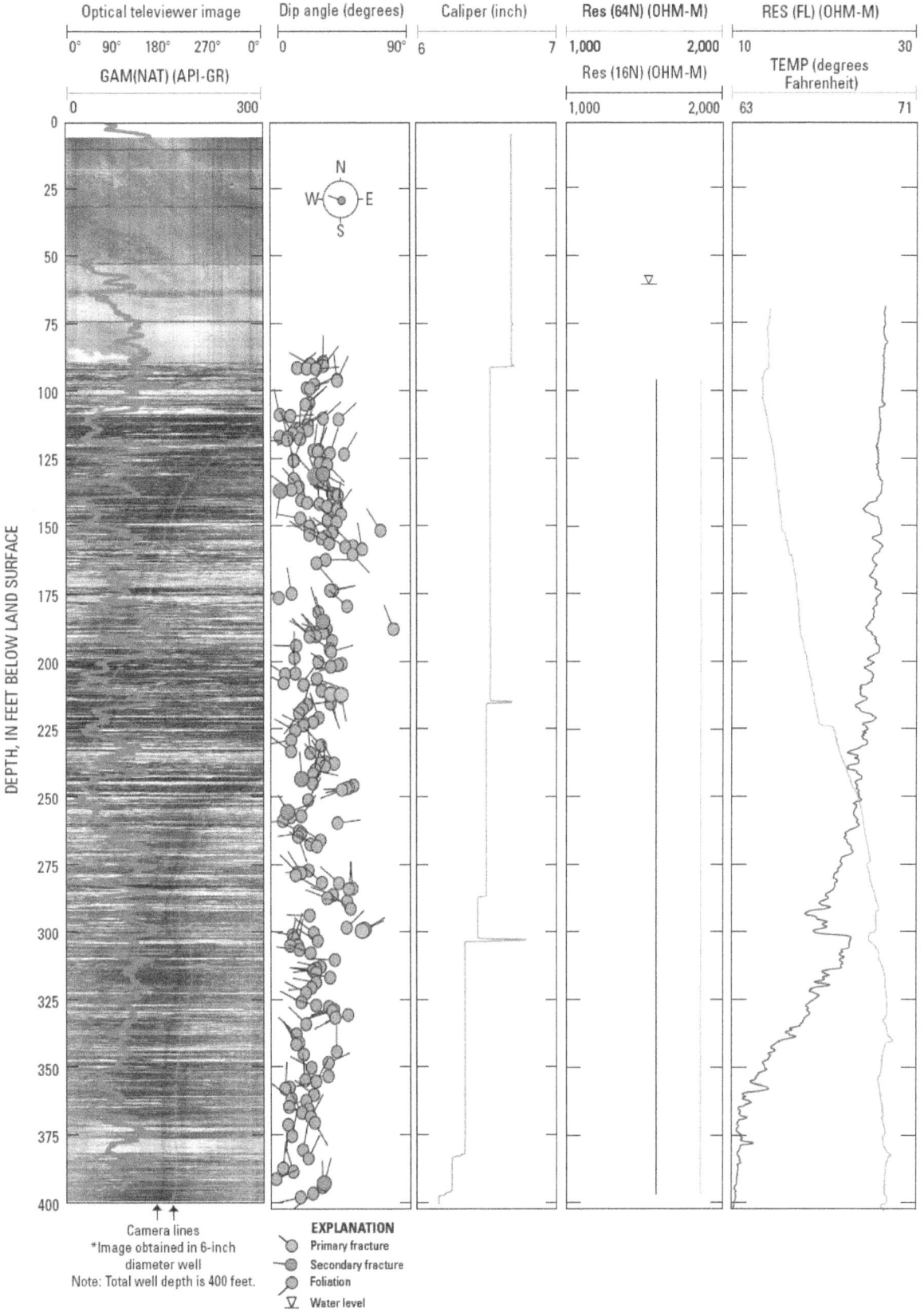

Figure 7.   Geophysical logs for bedrock well MW-1D at the Allison Woods research station, North Carolina.

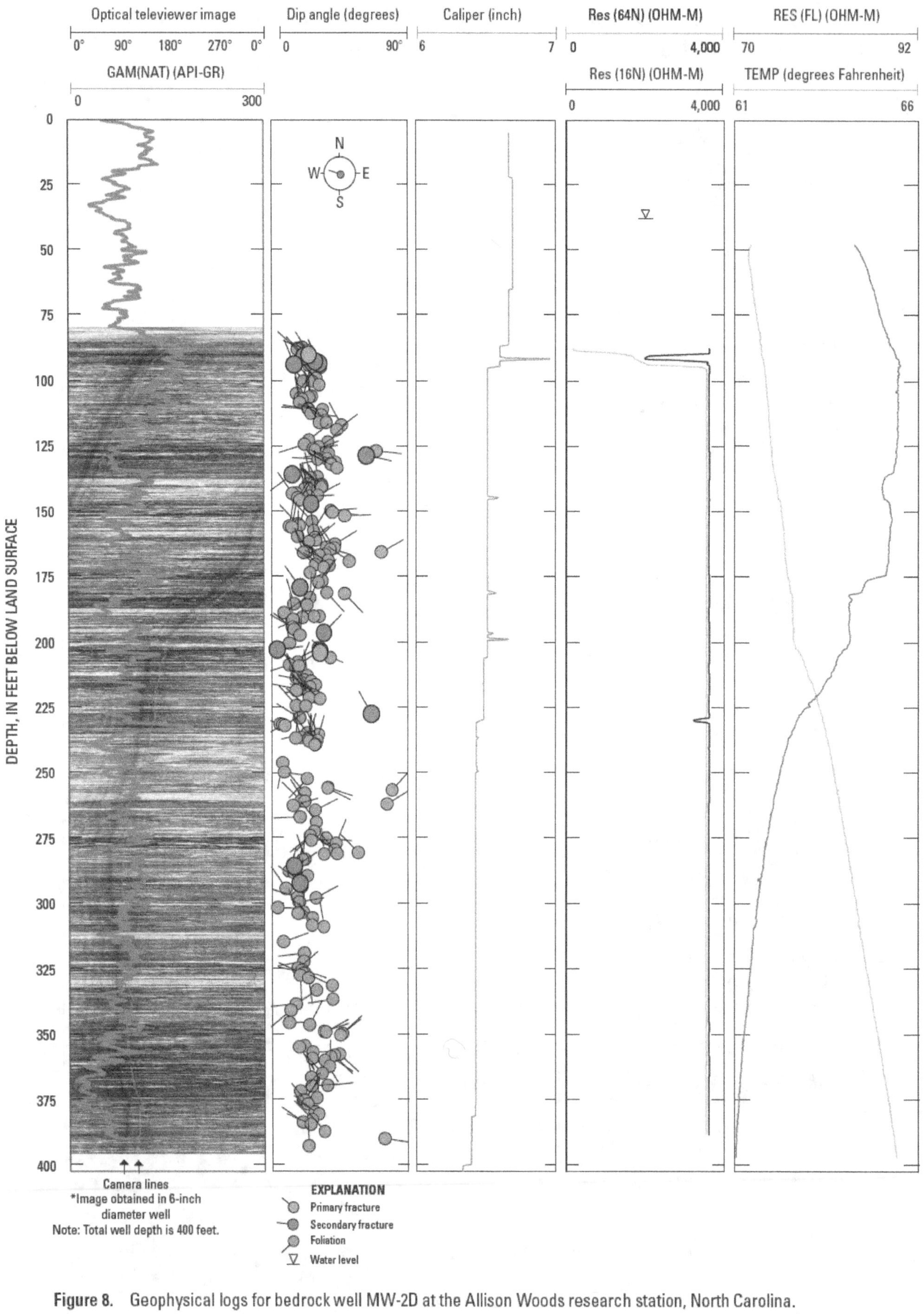

Figure 8. Geophysical logs for bedrock well MW-2D at the Allison Woods research station, North Carolina.

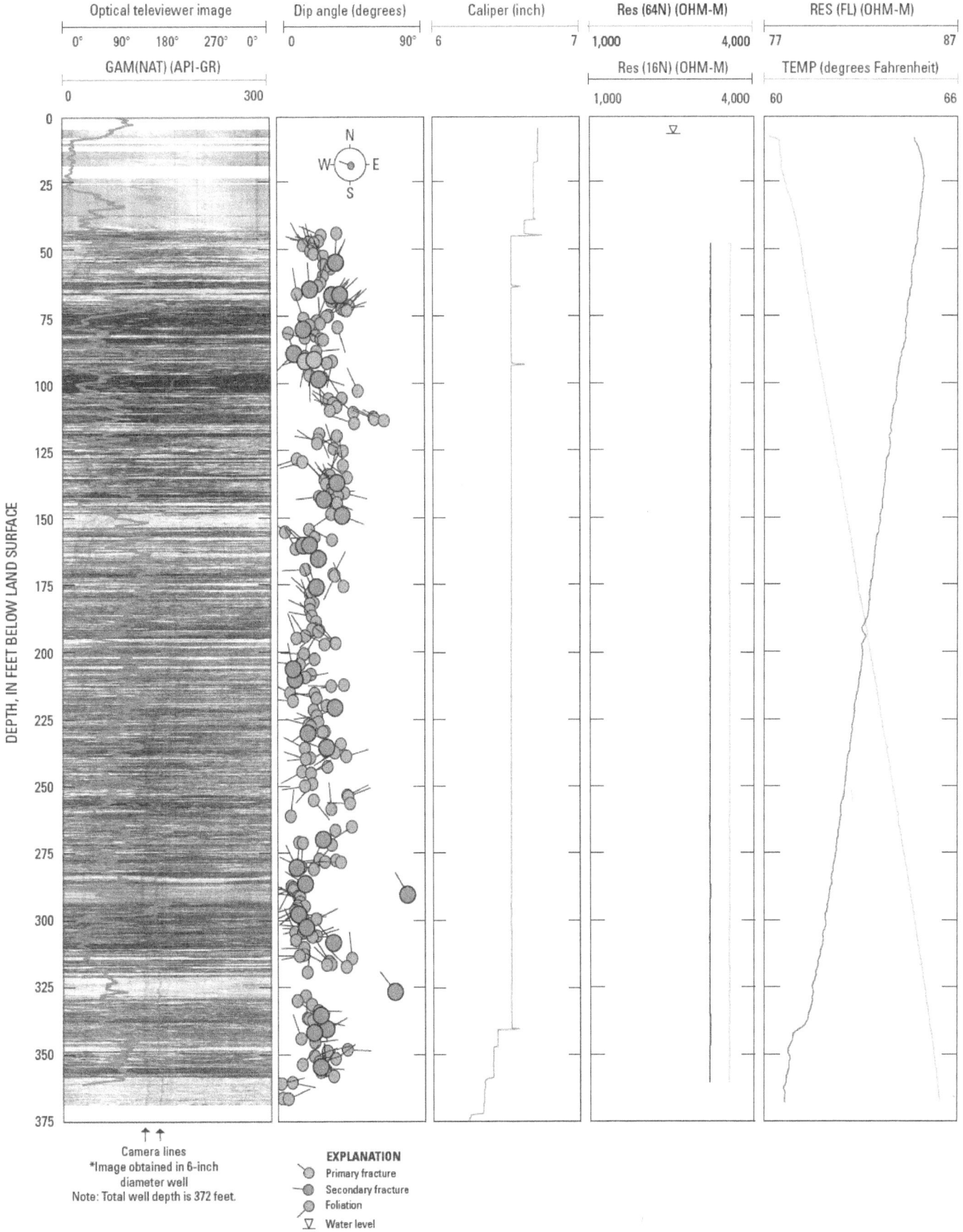

Figure 9. Geophysical logs for bedrock well MW-3D at the Allison Woods research station, North Carolina.

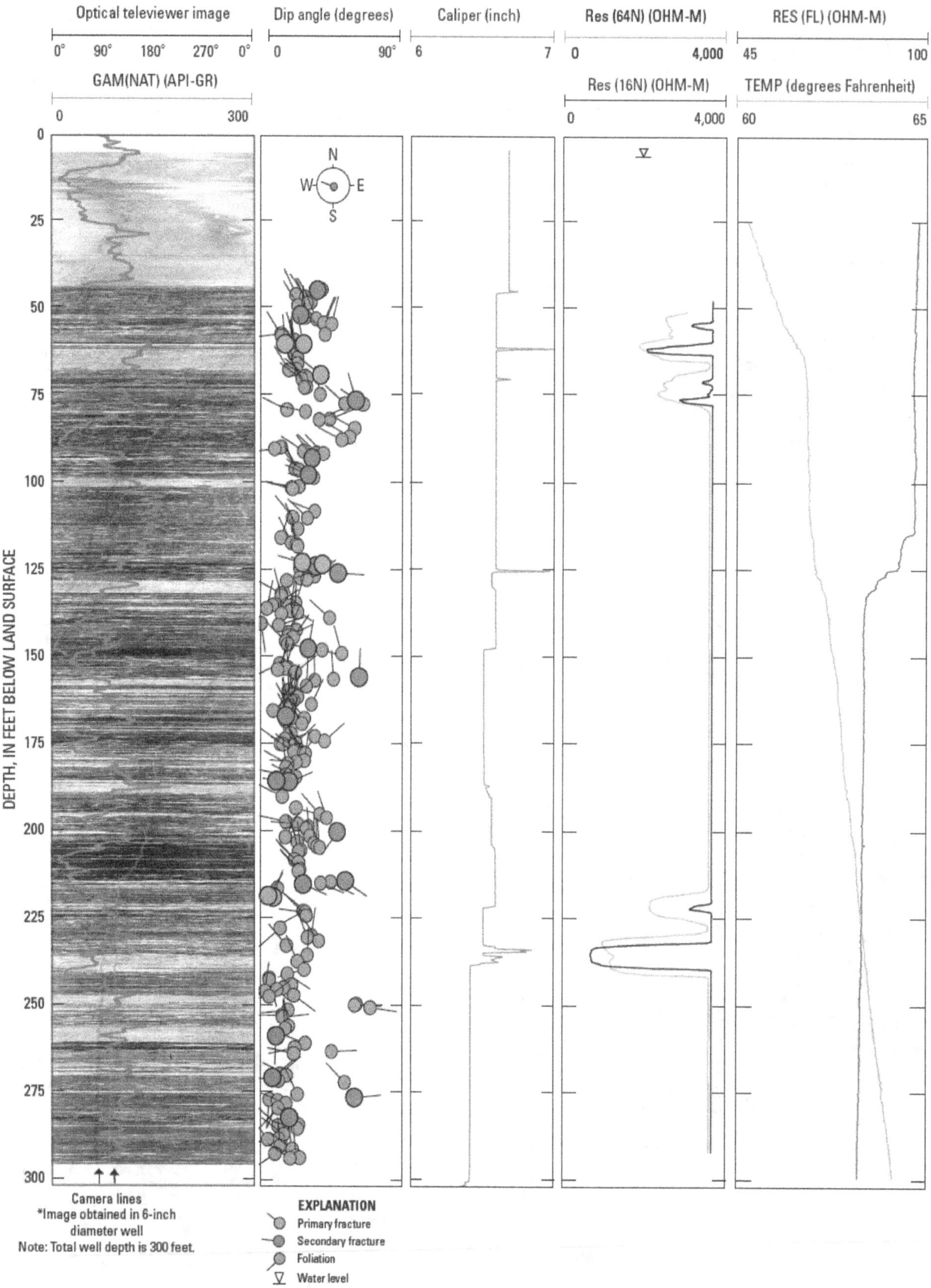

Figure 10.   Geophysical logs for bedrock well MW-4D at the Allison Woods research station, North Carolina.

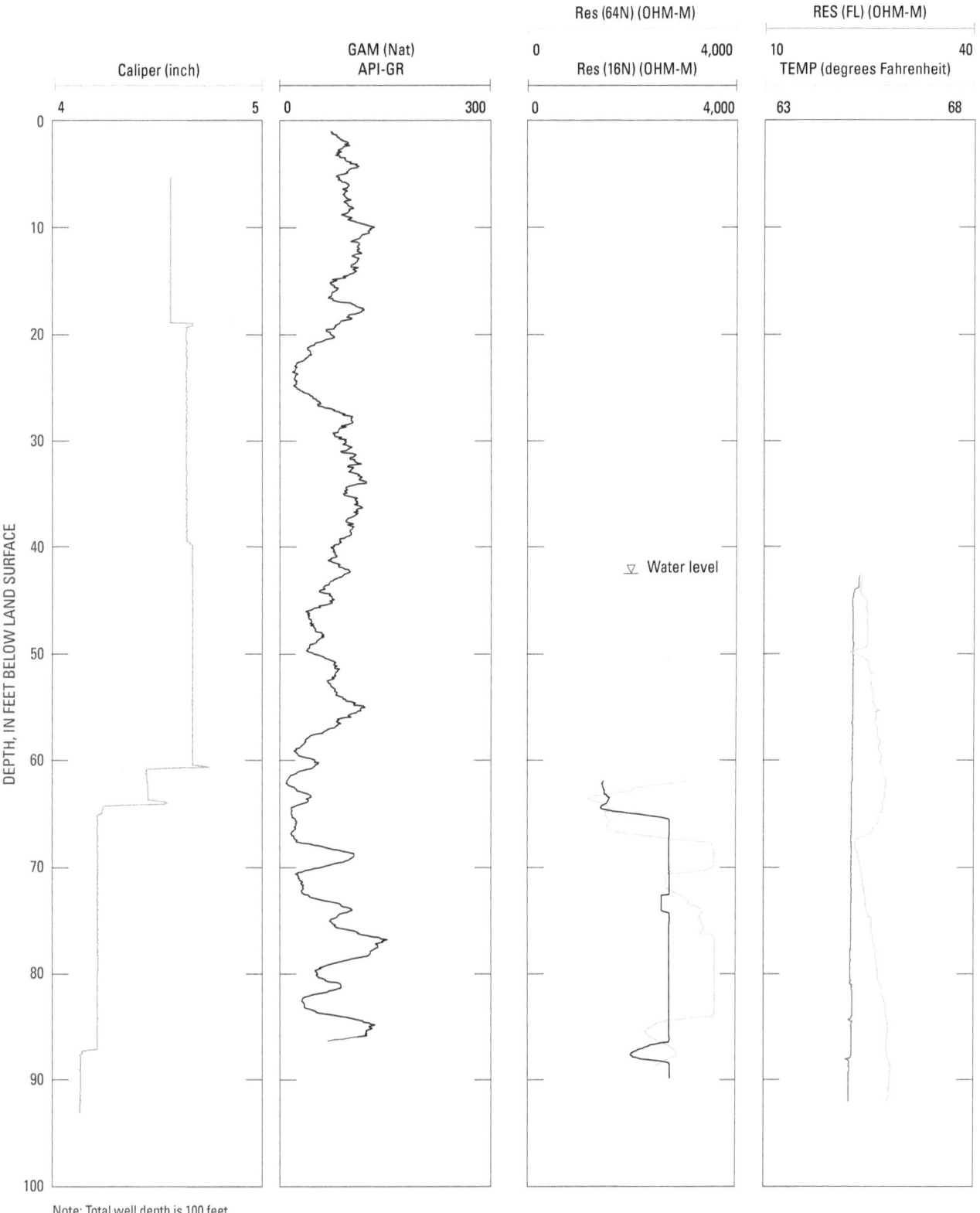

Figure 11.   Geophysical logs for corehole well CH-1 at the Allison Woods research station, North Carolina.

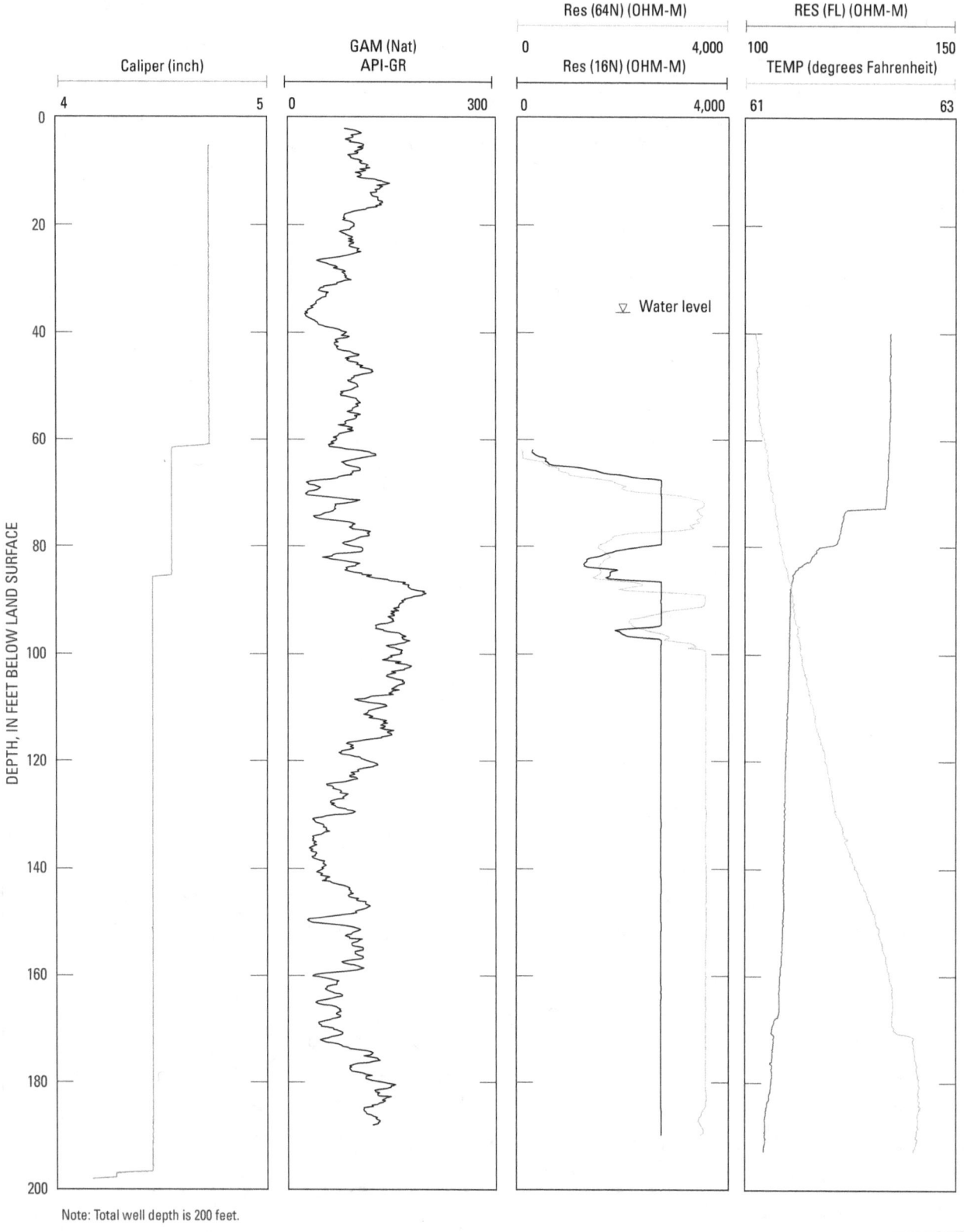

Note: Total well depth is 200 feet.

Figure 12. Geophysical logs for corehole well CH-2 at the Allison Woods research station, North Carolina.

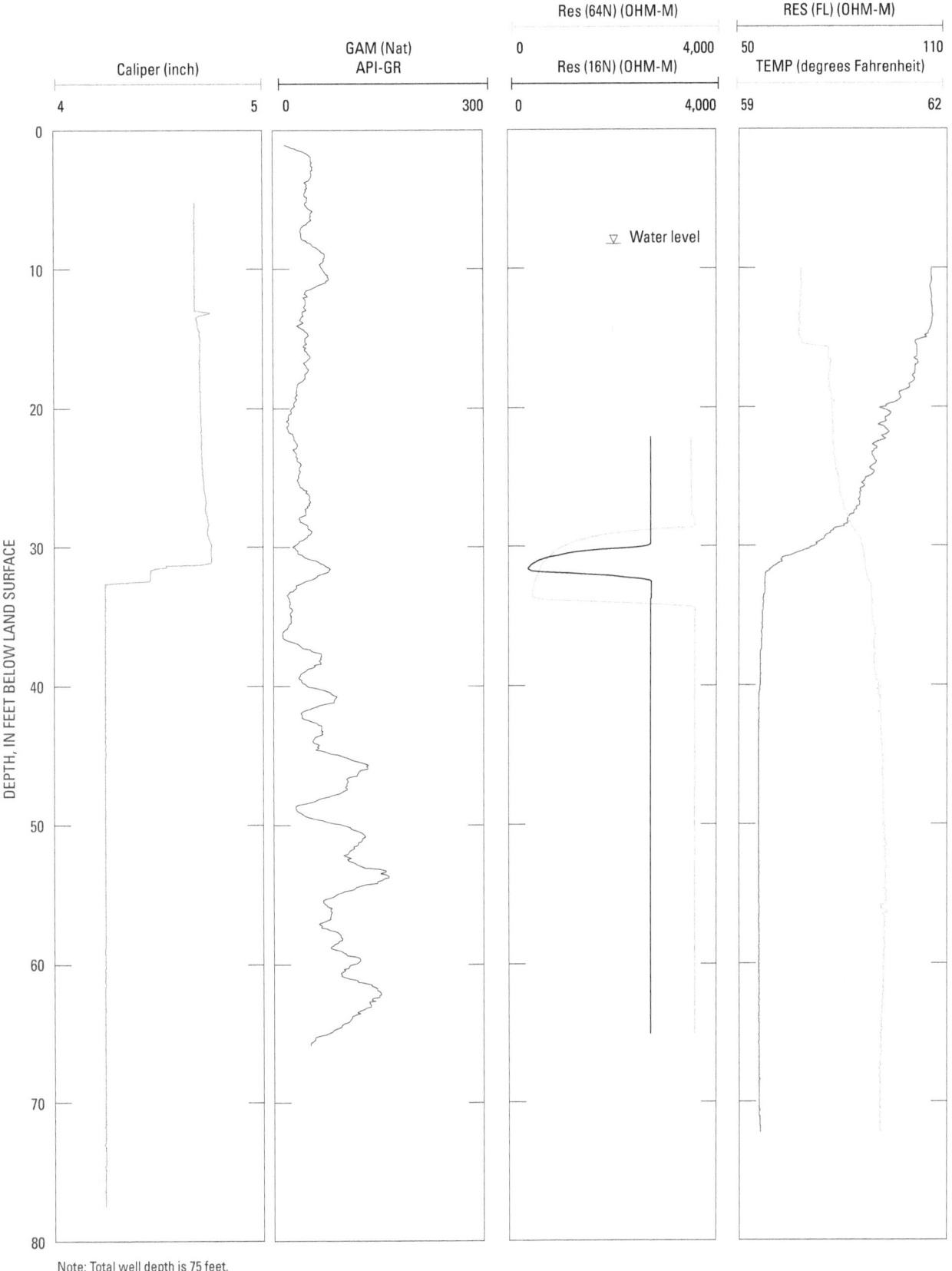

Figure 13.   Geophysical logs for corehole well CH-3 at the Allison Woods research station, North Carolina.

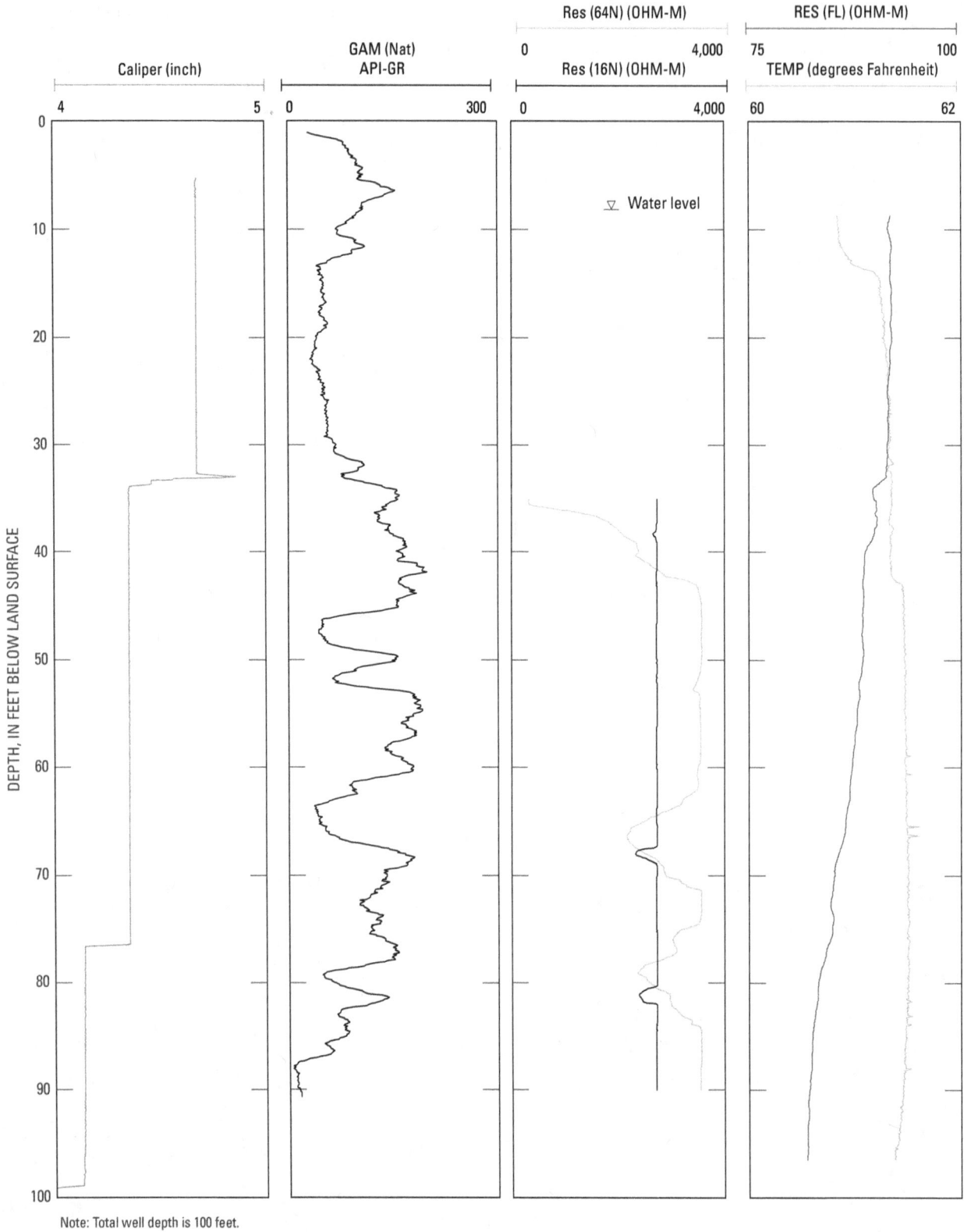

Note: Total well depth is 100 feet.

Figure 14.   Geophysical logs for corehole well CH-4 at the Allison Woods research station, North Carolina.

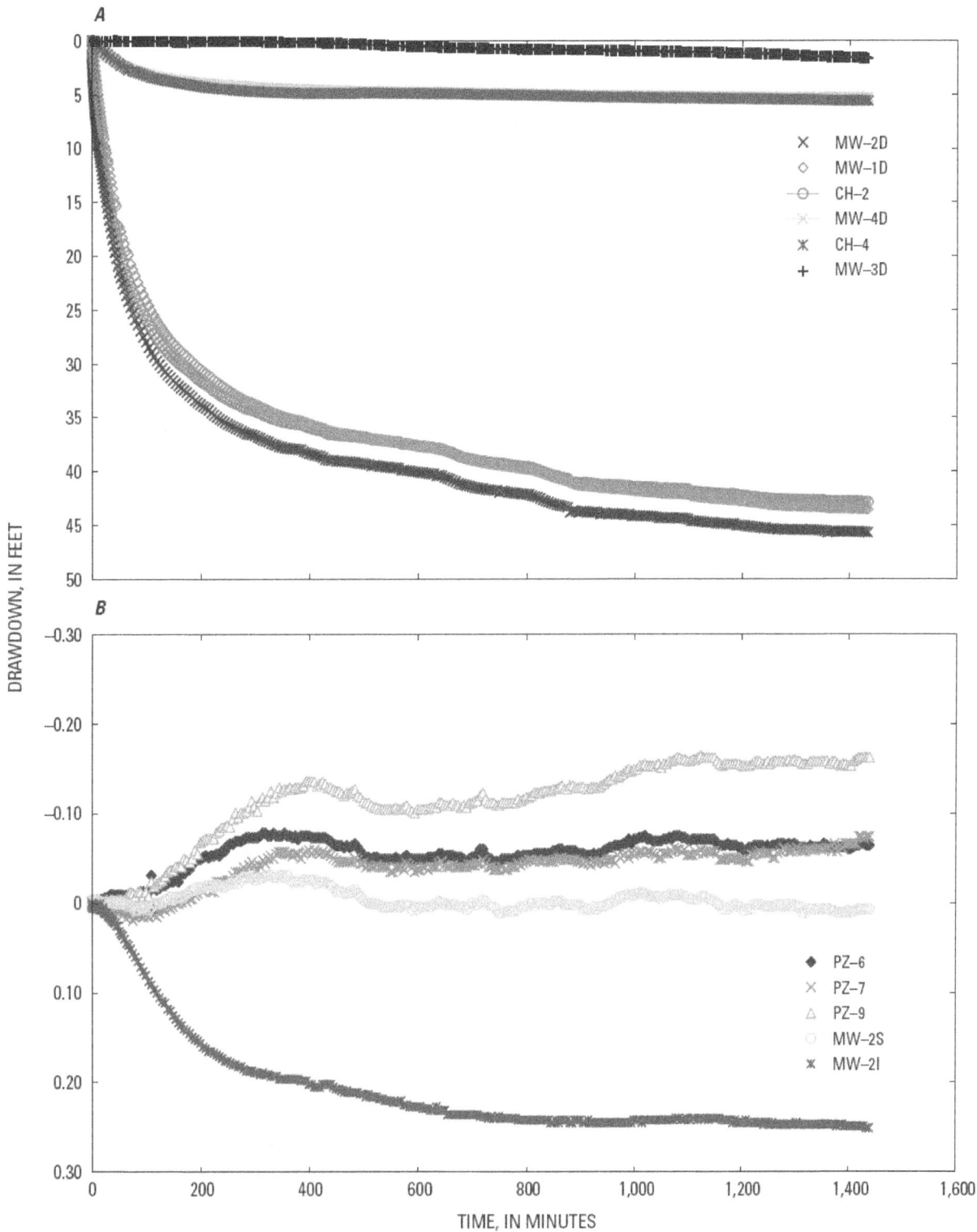

Figure 15.   Time-drawdown response of pumped well (MW-2D) and select observation wells measured during the October 2007 aquifer test in *(A)* bedrock wells and coreholes and *(B)* piezometers, a shallow regolith well, and a transition-zone well located closest to the pumped well at the Allison Woods research station, North Carolina.

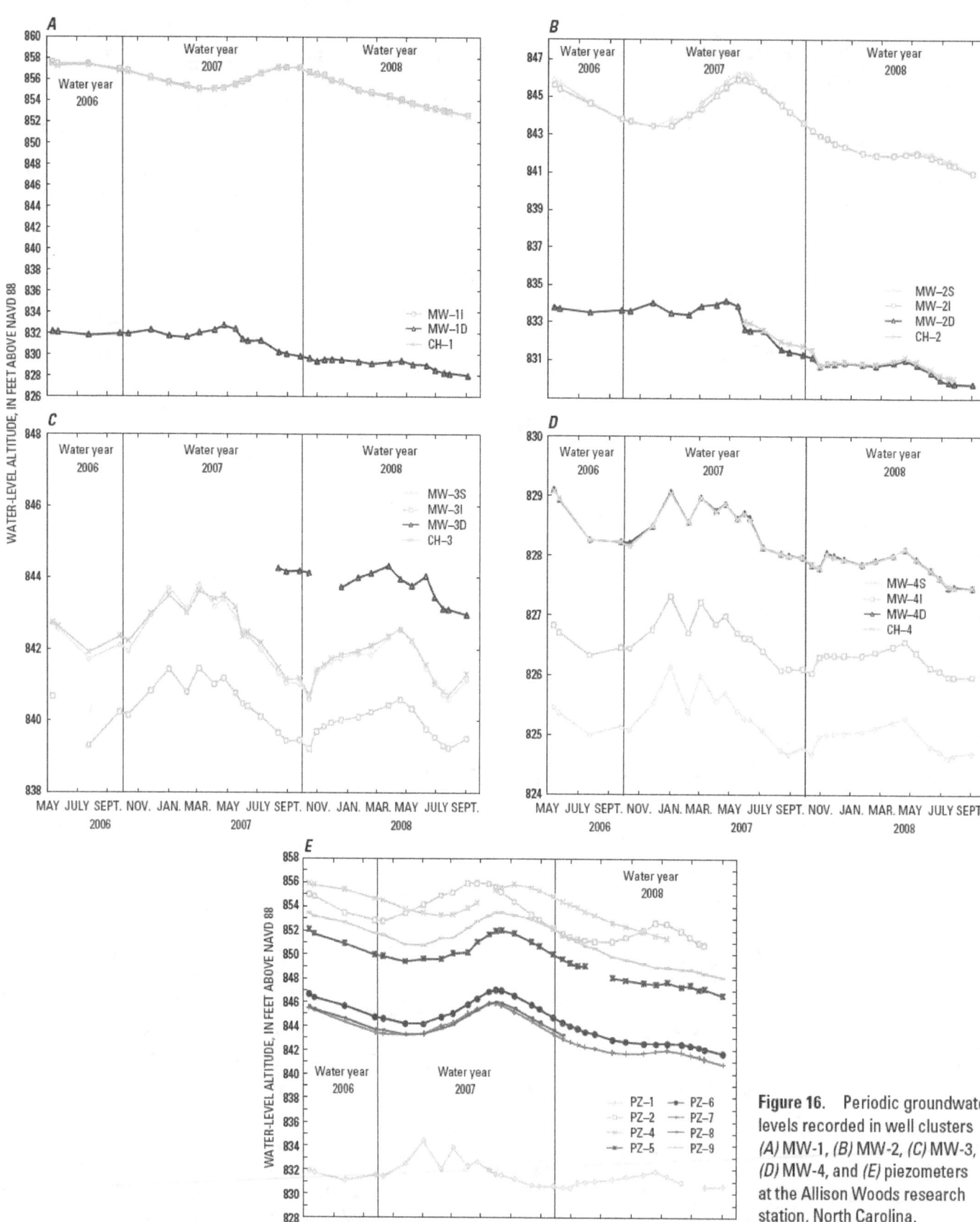

Figure 16. Periodic groundwater levels recorded in well clusters *(A)* MW-1, *(B)* MW-2, *(C)* MW-3, *(D)* MW-4, and *(E)* piezometers at the Allison Woods research station, North Carolina.

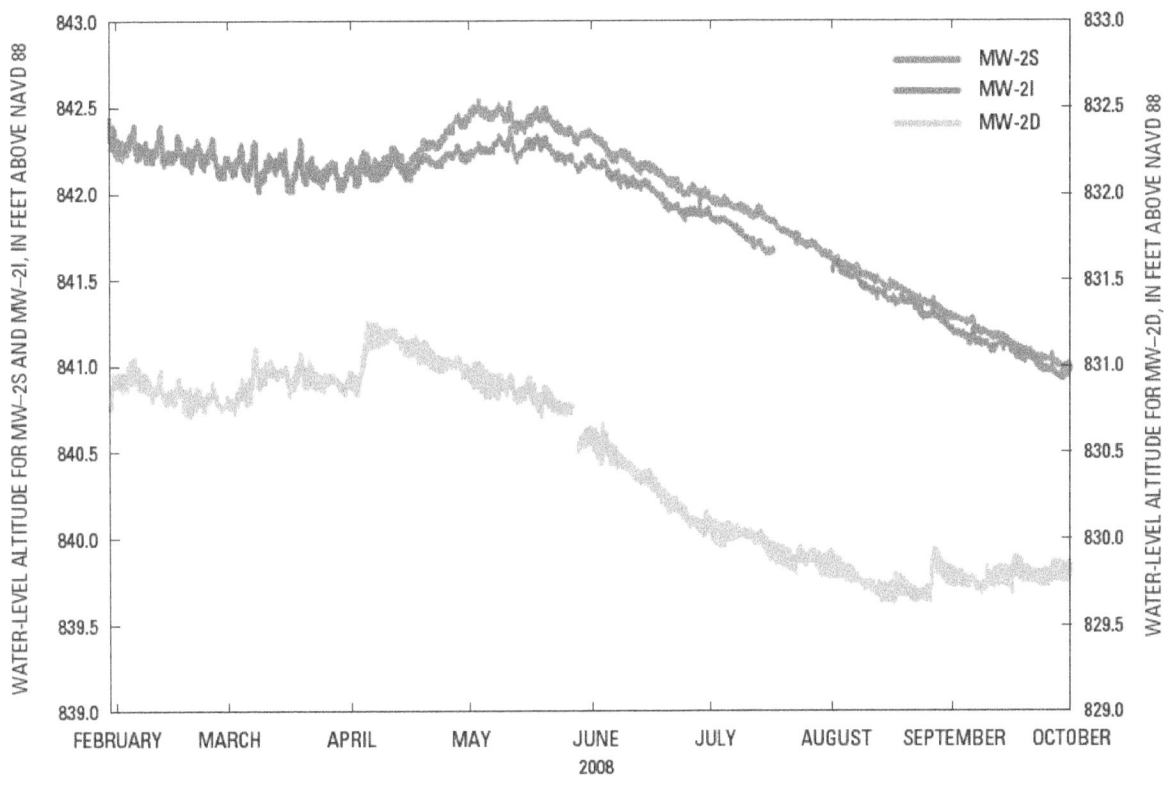

Figure 17. Hourly groundwater levels recorded in well cluster MW-2 at the Allison Woods research station, North Carolina, February through September 2008.

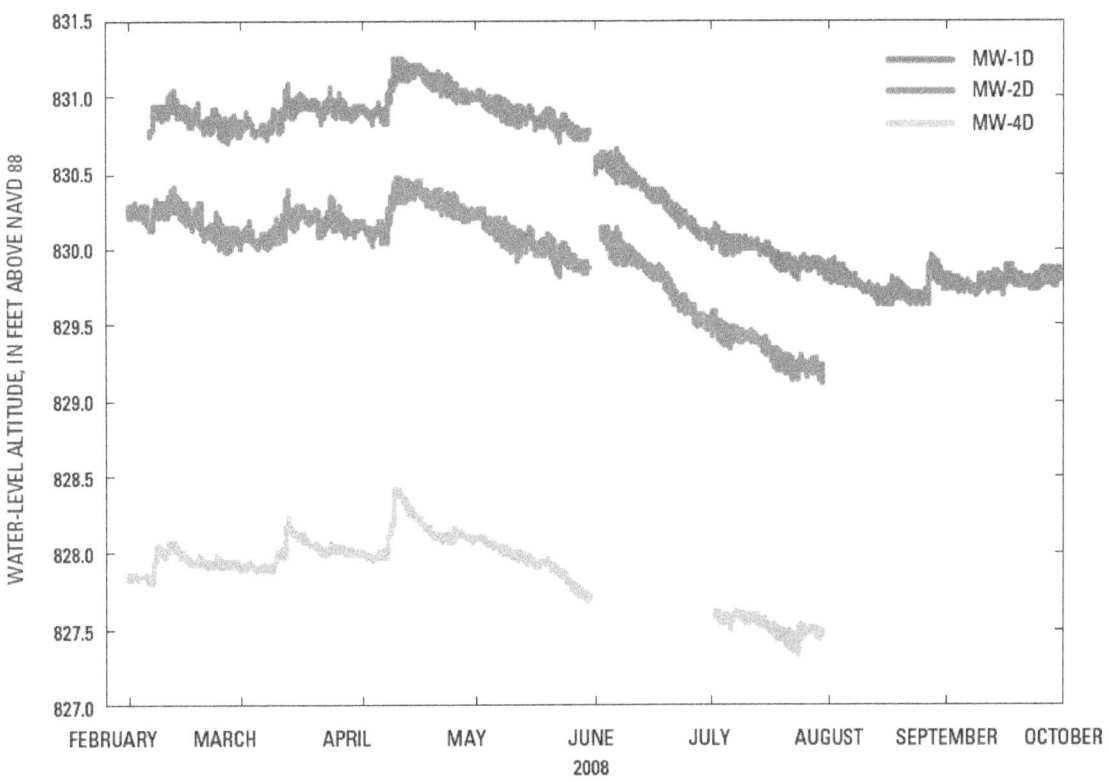

Figure 18. Hourly groundwater levels recorded in well clusters MW-1D, MW2-D, and MW-4D at the Allison Woods research station, North Carolina, February through September 2008.

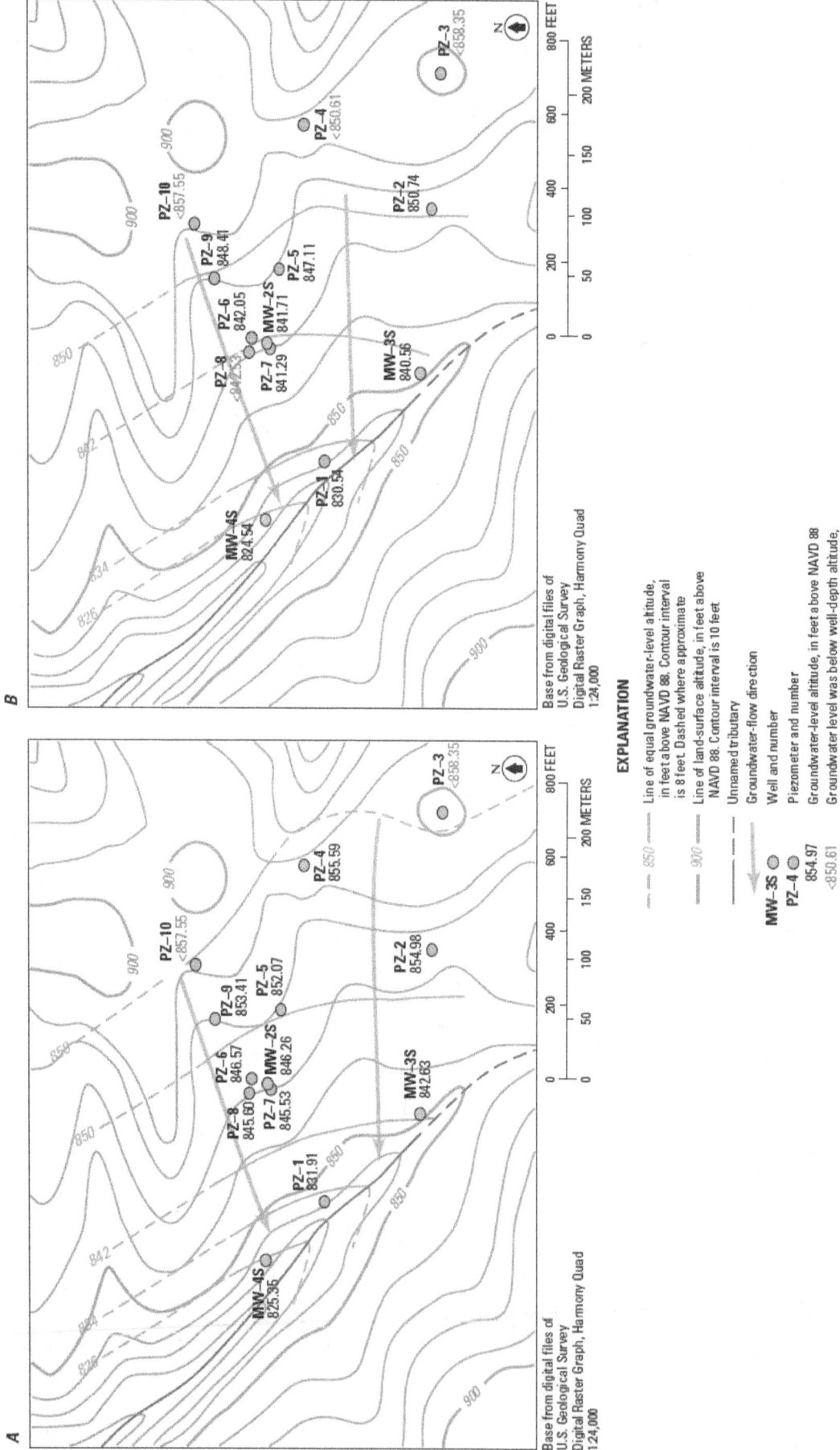

Figure 19. Water-level altitudes measured in the shallow regolith at the Allison Woods research station, North Carolina, for *(A)* May 12, 2006 (near maximum), and *(B)* July 29, 2008 (near minimum).

Results of two sampling events that were conducted in November 2006 and July 2007 and analyzed by the USGS National Water Quality laboratory are provided in this report (Appendix 2). Samples were collected from most of the wells (excluding piezometers). The unnamed tributary (USGS station 02117495) was sampled once in July 2007. MW-1S was not sampled because of low water levels (dry). Not all constituents discussed in the Methods of Data Collection section were analyzed following each sampling event. Radon 222 (gas) was analyzed following the July 2007 sampling event only. Bedrock wells—MW-1D, MW-3D, and MW-4D—have high pH (> 8.0), possibly due to grout contamination. Therefore, selected water-quality parameters from these three bedrock wells are excluded from this report.

Results of the water-quality data collected are displayed in Piper diagrams (fig. 20) and in Stiff diagrams (fig. 21). Ranges in values of physical properties in periodic water-quality samples are shown in figure 22, and ranges in major ion concentrations are shown in figures 23 and 24. Water-quality results for two sample sets (November 2006 and July 2007) are included in Appendix 2.

Water-quality field parameters were recorded at hourly intervals in three wells in cluster MW-2 (MW-2S, MW-2I, and MW-2D) at the AWRS from January 2008 through September 2008 (figs. 25–27). The field parameters recorded were temperature, pH, specific conductance, and dissolved oxygen. Water temperature at well cluster MW-2 ranged from about 14.0 to 14.2 degrees Celsius (°C) in the shallow zone. Water temperature was steady at 14.3 °C in the transition zone well and was steady at 14.5 °C in the bedrock zone. Specific conductance ranged from about 10 to 14 microsiemens per centimeter (μS/cm) at 25 °C in the shallow regolith zone, from about 52 to 88 μS/cm in the transition zone, and from about 137 to 150 μS/cm in the bedrock zone. The pH ranged from about 4.6 to 5.0 in the shallow regolith zone, from about 5.8 to 6.3 in the transition zone, and from about 7.0 to 7.2 in the bedrock zone. Dissolved oxygen ranged from about 7.5 to 9.3 mg/L in the shallow regolith zone, from about 0.0 to 1.2 mg/L in the transition zone, and from about 0.3 to 0.4 mg/L in the bedrock zone.

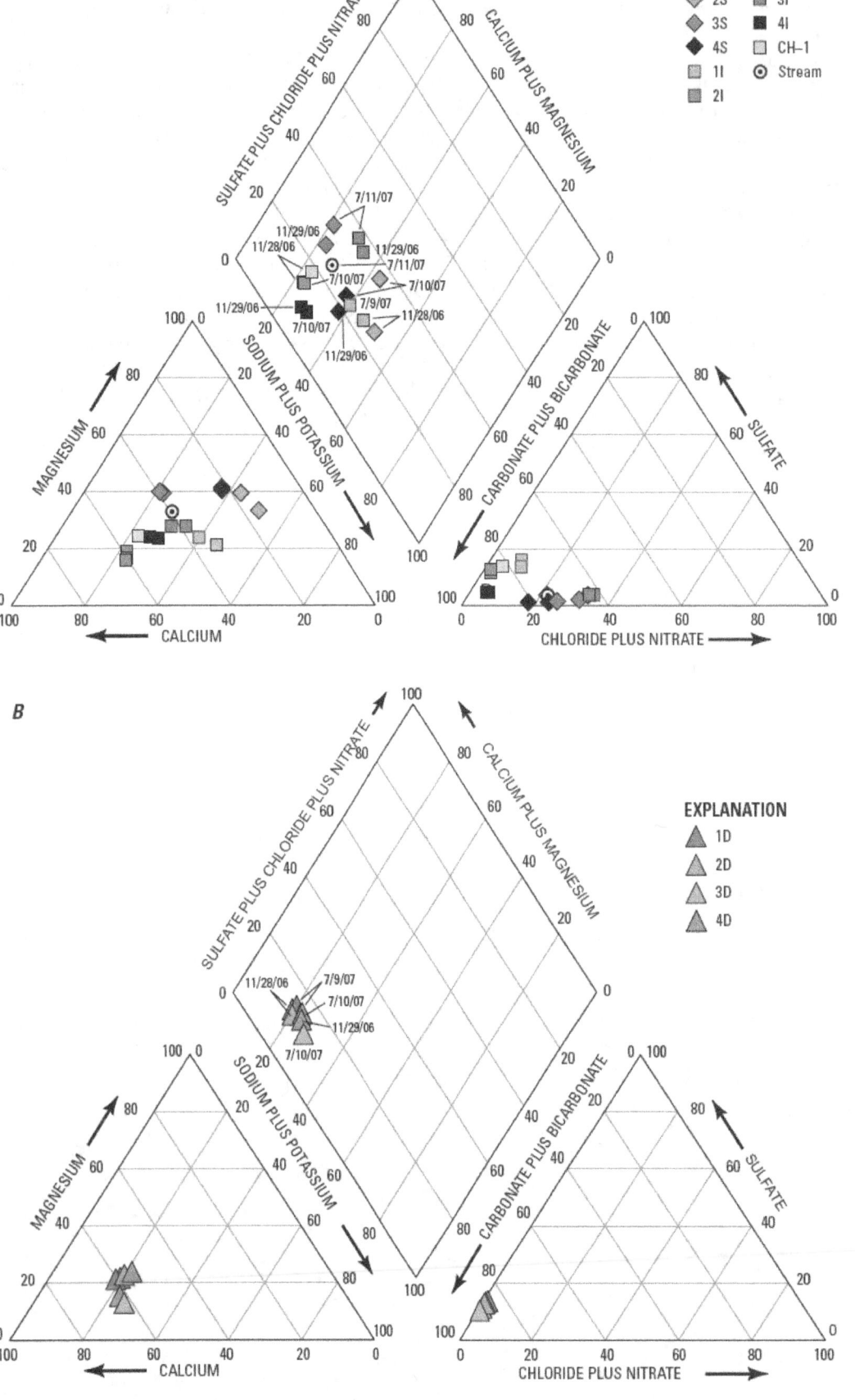

Figure 20. Piper diagrams showing distribution of major ion percentages in periodic groundwater samples from *(A)* the regolith and transition-zone wells and surface-water samples, and *(B)* the open-borehole bedrock wells.

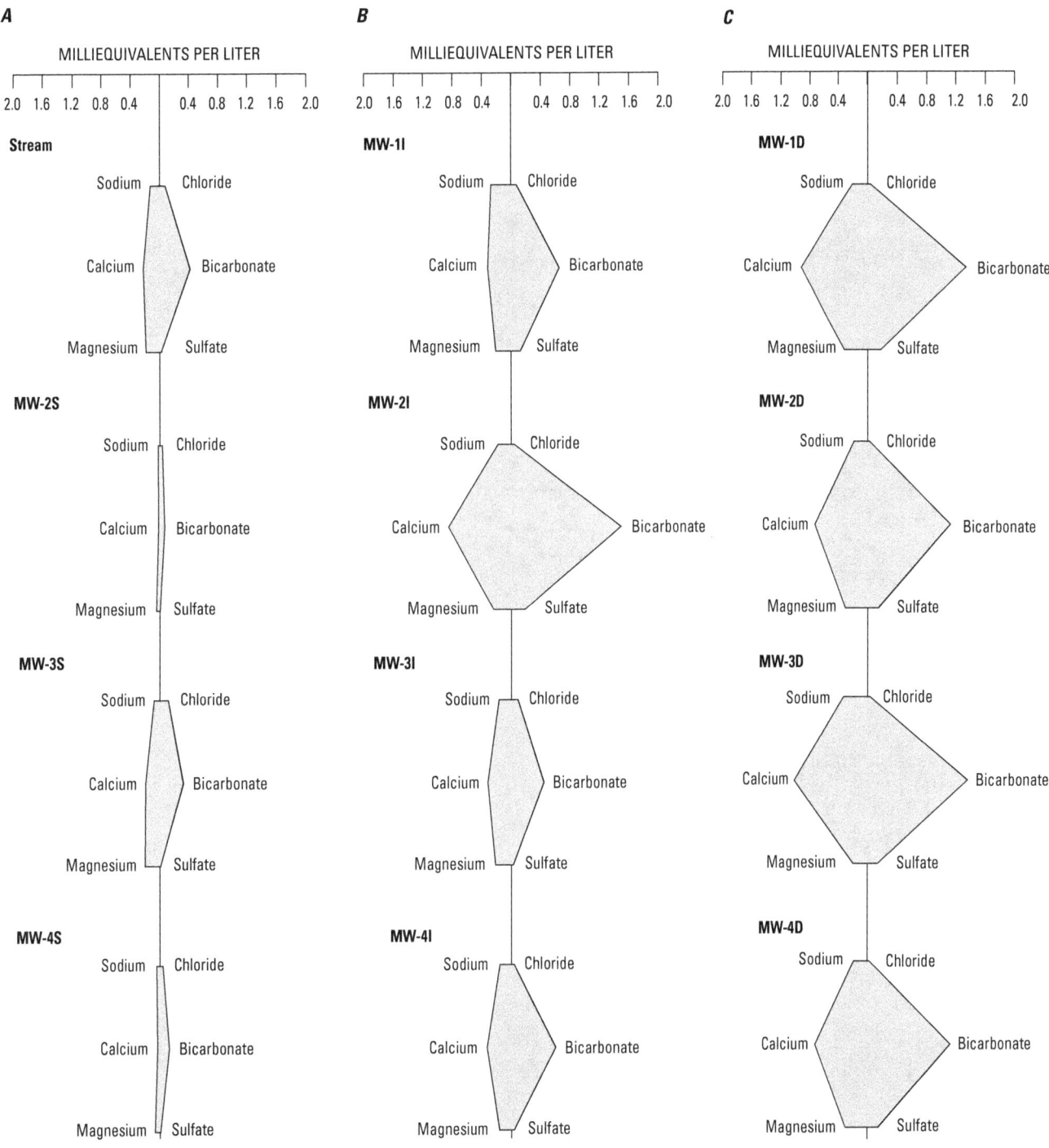

Figure 21. Major ion milliequivalents in water samples collected from *(A)* regolith wells and the stream, *(B)* transition-zone wells, and *(C)* open-borehole bedrock well MW-2D at the Allison Woods research station, North Carolina, July 2007.

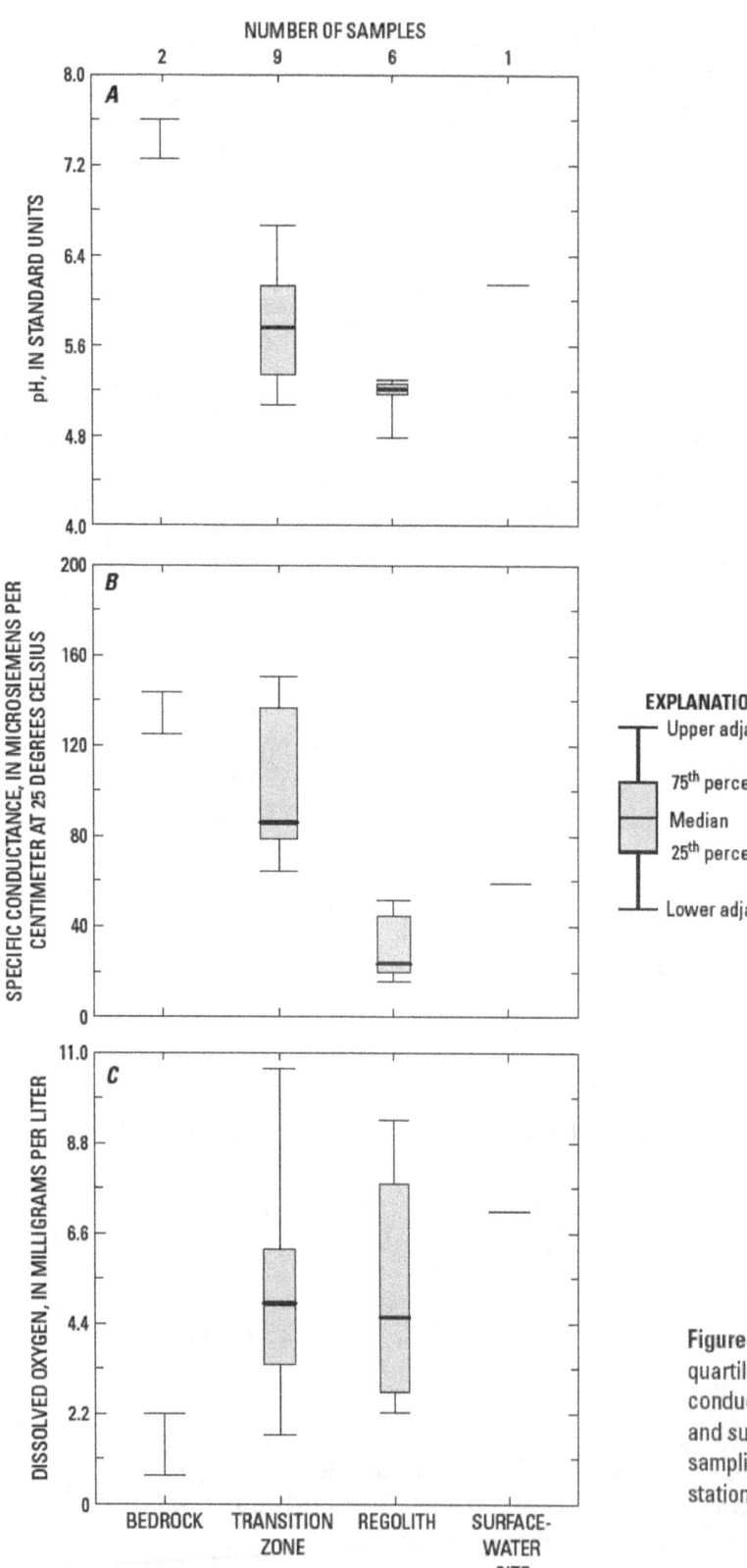

Figure 22. Box plots showing range, median, and quartile statistical values for *(A)* pH, *(B)* specific conductance, and *(C)* dissolved oxygen in the wells and surface-water site recorded during periodic sampling events at the Allison Woods research station, North Carolina.

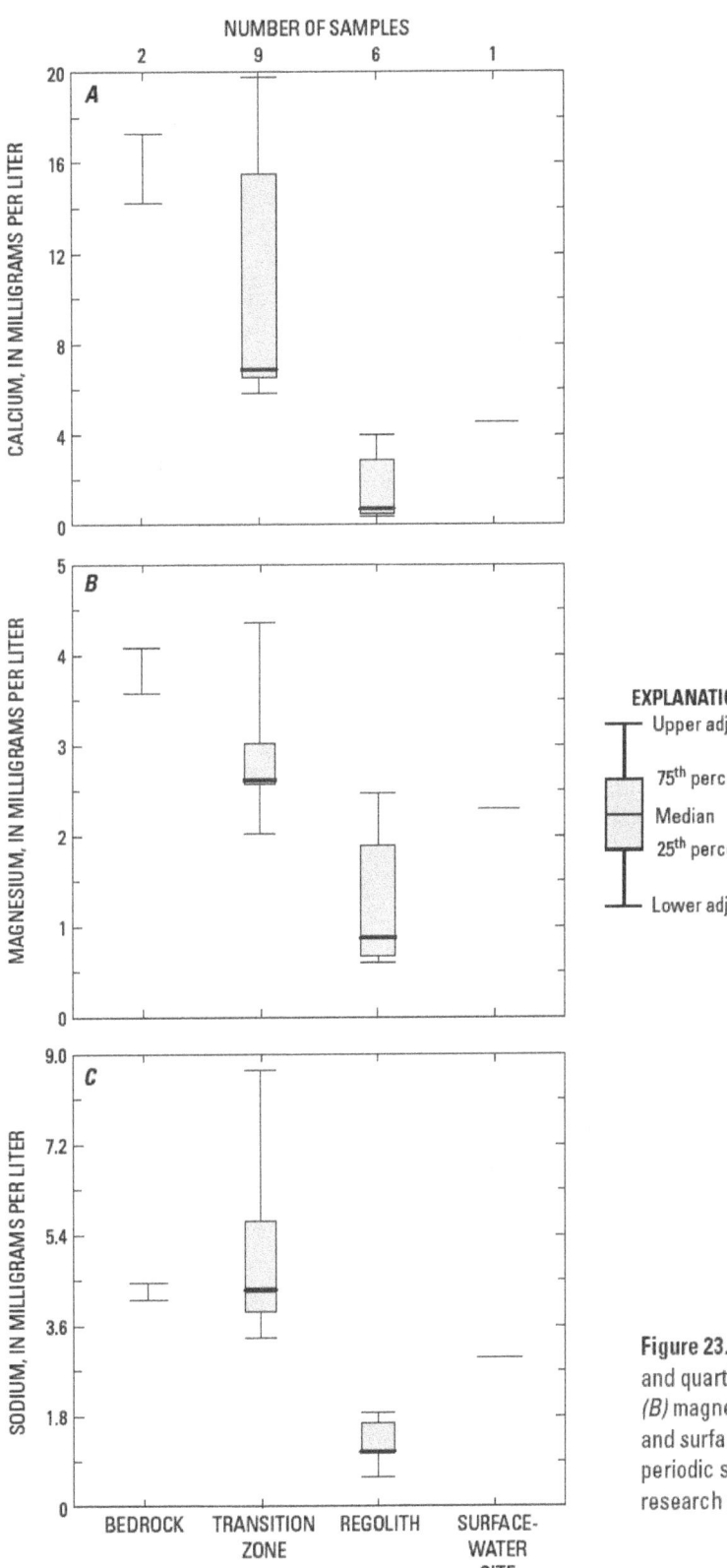

Figure 23.   Box plots showing range, median, and quartile statistical values for *(A)* calcium, *(B)* magnesium, and *(C)* sodium in the wells and surface-water site recorded during periodic sampling events at the Allison Woods research station, North Carolina.

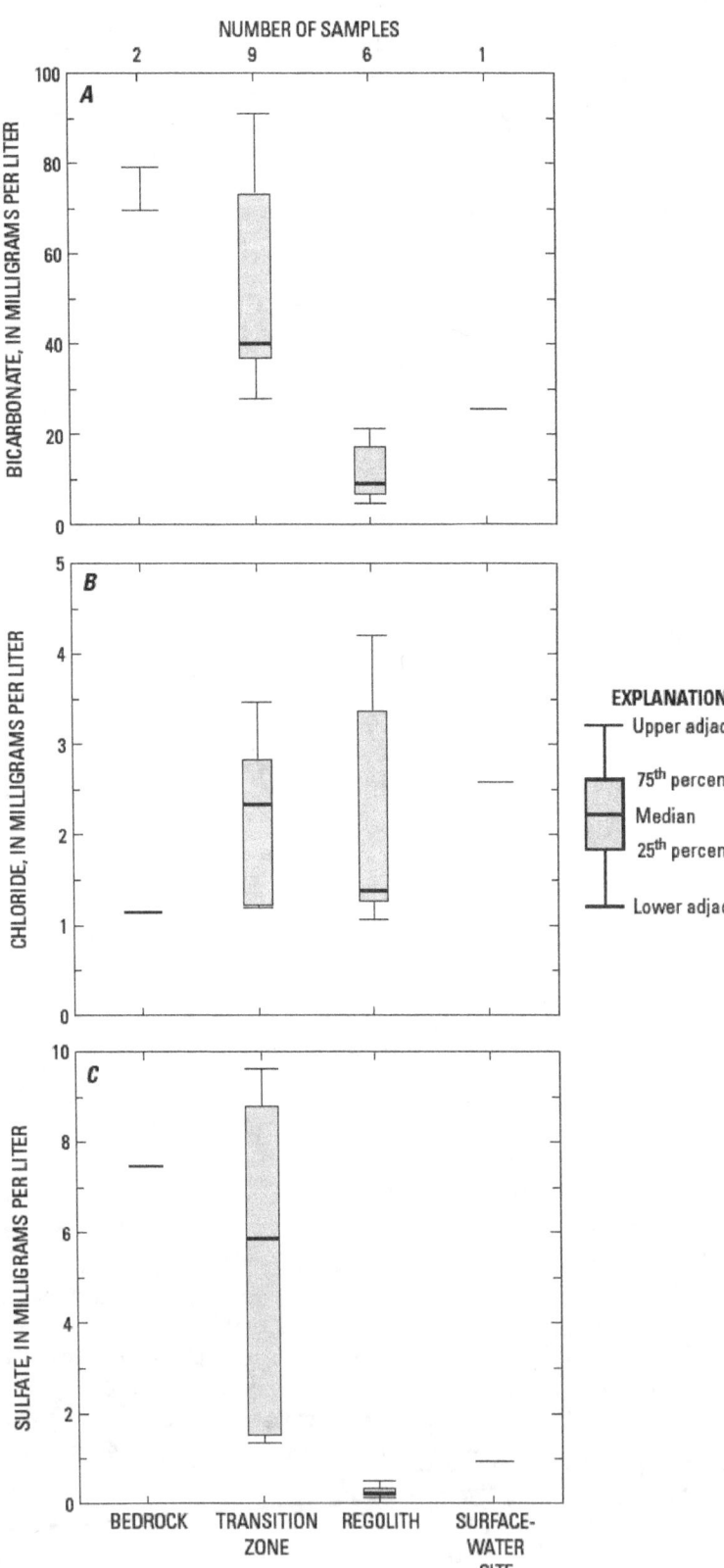

Figure 24. Box plots showing range, median, and quartile statistical values for *(A)* bicarbonate, *(B)* chloride, and *(C)* sulfate in the wells and surface-water site recorded during periodic sampling events at the Allison Woods research station, North Carolina.

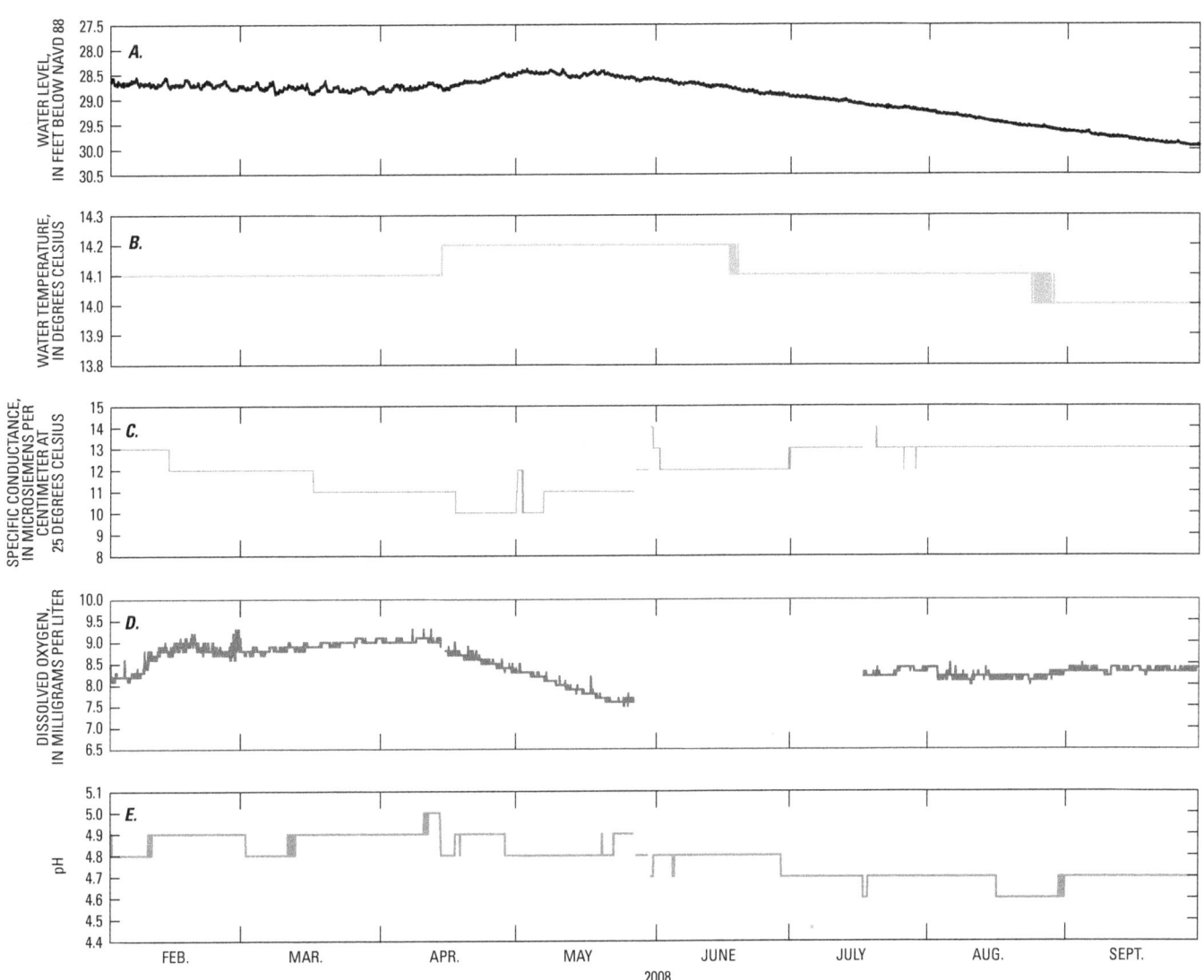

Figure 25.   Hourly record of *(A)* water level, *(B)* water temperature, *(C)* specific conductance, *(D)* dissolved oxygen, and *(E)* pH in well MW-2S in the shallow regolith at the Allison Woods research station, North Carolina.

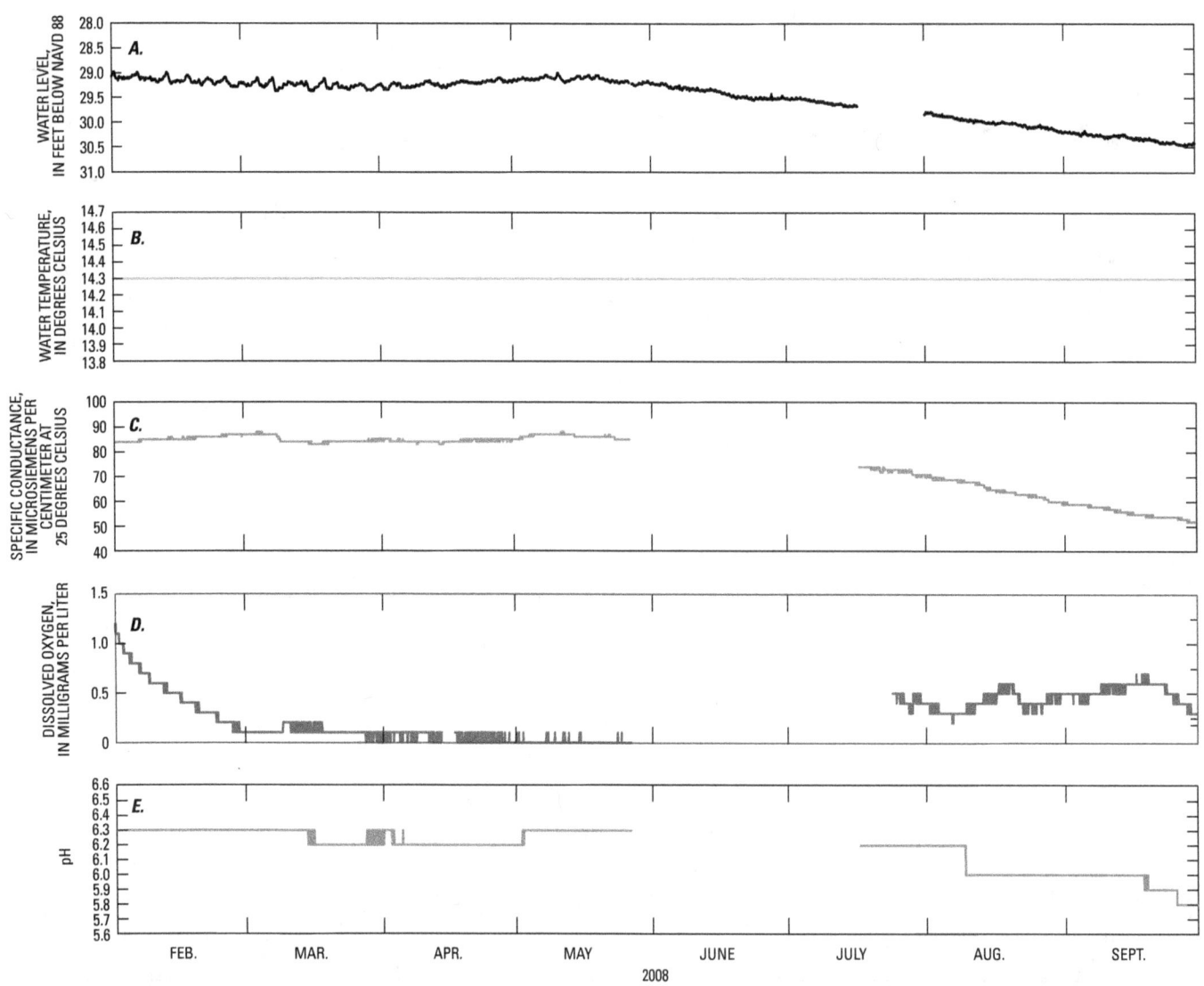

Figure 26   Hourly record of *(A)* water level, *(B)* water temperature, *(C)* specific conductance, *(D)* dissolved oxygen, and *(E)* pH in well MW-2I in the shallow regolith at the Allison Woods research station, North Carolina.

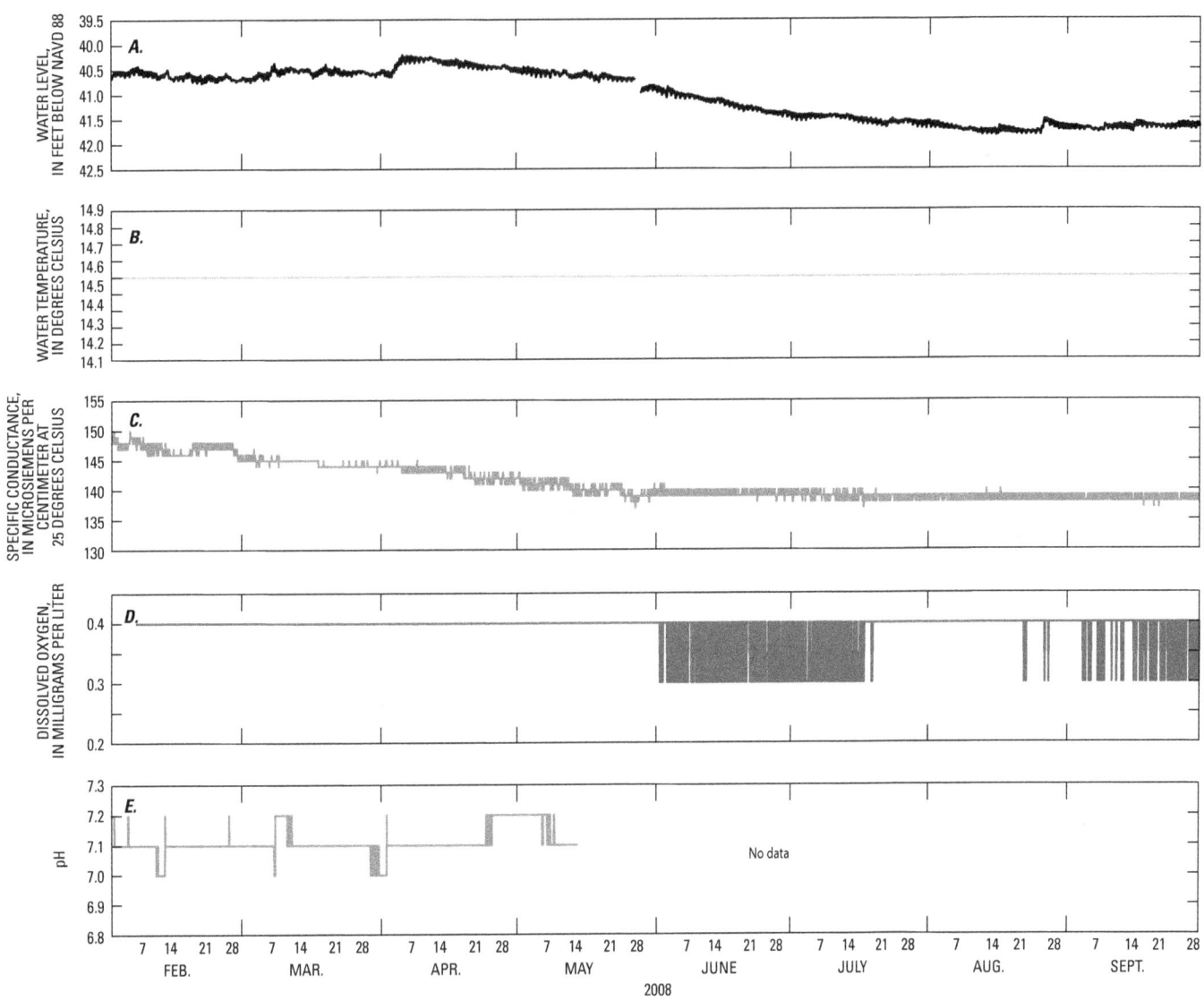

Figure 27.   Hourly record of *(A)* water level, *(B)* water temperature, *(C)* specific conductance, *(D)* dissolved oxygen, and *(E)* pH in well MW-2D in the shallow regolith at the Allison Woods research station, North Carolina.

Summary

Water-resources data were collected to describe the hydrologic conditions and water quality at the Allison Woods research station (AWRS) located near Statesville in the Piedmont Physiographic Province of North Carolina. As a part of this investigation, four continuous soil-bedrock cores were collected, and 29 wells were established at the AWRS. This report provides the well-construction details, periodic groundwater-level measurements for 29 wells, continuous (hourly) groundwater-level measurements for 5 wells, shallow groundwater-flow maps, borehole geophysical logs for 8 wells, continuous water-quality measurements for 3 wells, periodic water-quality data for 12 wells and 1 surface-water station, and slug-test results for 11 wells. The geology and hydrogeology of the site are also summarized. This report provides field and laboratory data collected from April 2005 through September 2008.

Acknowledgments

The authors thank the board members and manager of the Allison Woods Foundation for providing access to the property to conduct this study. Their cooperation in making this study possible is appreciated. The authors thank Charles G. Pippin, formerly with NCDENR-DWQ, who managed the initial part of this project, including geologic coring and well construction. Thanks to all the members of the NCDENR/USGS Piedmont and Mountains Resource Evaluation Program who continually contributed to data collection and interpretation during this project. These members include Melinda Chapman, Cassandra Pfeifle, and Kristen McSwain of the U.S. Geological Survey; Andrew Pitner of the Mooresville DWQ Regional Office; Richard E. Bolich, Evan Kane, and Ray Milosh of the Raleigh DWQ Central Office; Ted R. Campbell of the Asheville DWQ Regional Office; Shuying Wang of the Winston-Salem DWQ Regional Office; and Lori Skidmore of the Raleigh Regional Office of the NCDENR. Thanks to the NCDENR-DWQ drillers for the hard work, perseverance, and patience they displayed in dealing with conditions in the field and their willingness to do whatever was necessary to complete the work.

References

Bouwer, H., and Rice, R.C., 1976, A slug test for determining hydraulic conductivity of unconfined aquifers with completely or partially penetrating wells: Water Resources Research, v. 12, no. 3, p. 423–428.

Chapman, M.J., Bolich, R.E., and Huffman, B.A., 2005, Hydrogeologic setting, ground-water flow, and ground-water quality at the Lake Wheeler Road research station, 2001–03, North Carolina Piedmont and Blue Ridge Mountains Resource Evaluation Program: U.S. Geological Survey Scientific Investigations Report 2005–5166, 85 p.

Daniel, C.C., III, and Dahlen, P.R., 2002, Preliminary hydrogeologic assessment and study plan for a regional ground-water resource investigation of the Blue Ridge and Piedmont Provinces of North Carolina: U.S. Geological Survey Water-Resources Investigations Report 02-4105, 60 p., accessed November 2004 at *http://nc.water.usgs.gov/reports/wri024105/*.

Daniel, C.C., III, and Payne, R.A., 1990, Hydrogeologic unit map of the Piedmont and Blue Ridge Provinces of North Carolina: U.S. Geological Survey Water-Resources Investigations Report 90–4035, 1 map sheet, scale 1:500,000.

Goldsmith, Richard, Milton, D.J., and Horton, J.W., 1988, Geologic map of the Charlotte 1 degree by 2 degrees Quadrangle, North and South Carolina: U.S. Geological Survey IMAP 1251-E, 1 sheet.

Halford, K.J., and Kuniansky, E.L., 2002, Documentation of spreadsheets for the analysis of aquifer-test and slug-test data: U.S. Geological Survey Open-File Report 02–197, 54 p.

Harned, D.A., and Daniel, C.C., III, 1992, The transition zone between bedrock and saprolite—Conduit for contamination? *in* Daniel, C.C., III, White, R.K., and Stone, P.A., eds., Ground water in the Piedmont of the Eastern United States: Clemson, S.C., Clemson University, p. 336–348.

Heath, R.C., 1980, Basic elements of ground-water hydrology with reference to conditions in North Carolina: U.S. Geological Survey Open-File Report 80-44, 86 p.

Hibbard, J.A., 2000, Docking Carolina, Mid-Paleozoic accretion in the southern Appalachians: Geology, v. 28, p. 127–130.

Hibbard, J.P., Stoddard, E.F., Secor, D.T. and Dennis, A.J., 2002, The Carolina Zone, Overview of Neoproterozoic to Early Paleozoic peri-Goldwanan terranes along the eastern flank of the southern Appalachians: Earth Science Reviews, v. 57, p. 299–339.

Huffman, B.A., Pfeifle, C.A., Chapman, M.J., Bolich, R.E., Campbell, T.R., Geddes, D.J., Jr., and Pippin, C.G., 2006, Compilation of water-resources data and hydrogeologic setting for four research stations in the Piedmont and Blue Ridge Physiographic Provinces of North Carolina, 2000–2004: U.S. Geological Survey Open-File Report 2006-1168, 102 p.

LeGrand, H.E., and Nelson, P.F., 2004, A master conceptual model for hydrogeological site characterization in the Piedmont and Mountain region of North Carolina, A guidance manual: Raleigh, North Carolina Department of Environment and Natural Resources, Division of Water Quality, Groundwater Section, 50 p.

North Carolina Department of Environment and Natural Resources, Division of Water Quality, 2008a, Standard operating procedures for the groundwater research stations, North Carolina Piedmont and Mountains Groundwater Resource Evaluation Program, accessed August 2009 at *http://h2o.enr.state.nc.us/gwp/documents/GWREP_SOP-Draft_Apr_08.pdf.*

North Carolina Department of Environment and Natural Resources, Division of Water Quality, 2008b, Allison Woods Research Station water-quality data, North Carolina Piedmont and Mountains Groundwater Resource Evaluation Program, accessed August 2009 at *http://h2o.enr.state.nc.us/gwp/Summary_AllisonWoods.htm*

North Carolina Geological Survey, 1985, Geologic map of North Carolina: Raleigh, North Carolina Geological Survey, scale 1:500,000.

Piper, A.M., 1953, A graphic procedure in the geochemical interpretation of water analyses: U.S. Geological Survey, Ground-Water Chemistry Notes, no. 12, 14 p.

State Climate Office of North Carolina, 2008, NCCRONOS database, accessed September 2008 at *http://www.nc-climate.ncsu.edu/cronos/?station=318778.*

Stiff, H.A., Jr., 1951, The interpretation of chemical water analysis by means of patterns: Journal of Petroleum Technology, v. 3, p. 15–17.

U.S. Geological Survey, 2005, North Carolina water-use data tables, 2005, accessed October 23, 2008, at *http://nc.water.usgs.gov/wateruse/data/Data_Tables_2005.html.*

U.S. Geological Survey, 2007, Lowest streamflows in more than 100 years for some North Carolina rivers as drought worsens: North Carolina Water Science Center, news release, August 31, 2007, accessed October 30, 2009, at *http://www.ncdrought.org/press/usgs_20070831.pdf.*

U.S. Geological Survey, 2008a, Water-resources data for the United States, water year 2007: U.S. Geological Survey Water-Data Report WDR-US-2007, accessed September 1, 2008, at *http://pubs.water.usgs.gov/wdr2007.*

U.S. Geological Survey, 2008b, Water use in North Carolina, 2005, accessed October 30, 2009, at *http://nc.water.usgs.gov/infodata/wateruse.html.*

U.S. Geological Survey, 2009, Water-resources data for the United States, Water year 2008: U.S. Geological Survey Water-Data Report WDR-US-2008, accessed November 3, 2009, at *http://pubs .water.usgs.gov/wdr2008.*

Wilde, F.D., Radtke, D.B., Gibs, Jacob, and Iwatsubo, R.T., 1999, National field manual for the collection of water-quality data—Collection of water samples: U.S. Geological Survey Techniques of Water-Resources Investigations, book 9, chap. A4 [variously paged].

Wortman, G.L., Samson, S.D., and Hibbard, J.P., 1996, 2000, Precise U-Pb zircon constraints on the earliest magmatic history of the Carolina Terrane: The Journal of Geology, v. 108, p. 321–338.

Appendix 1.   Geologic Core Descriptions from the Allison Woods Research Station

Abbreviations Used in Appendix 1

Dry/Wet

D, dry

M, moist, but no visible water

W, wet

Dry Strength

N, none—The dry specimen crumbles into powder with mere pressure of handling.

L, low—The dry specimen crumbles into powder with some finger pressure.

M, medium—The dry specimen breaks into pieces or crumbles with considerable finger pressure.

H, high—The dry specimen cannot be broken with finger pressure. Specimen will break into pieces between thumb and a hard surface.

VH, very high—The dry specimen cannot be broken between the thumb and a hard surface.

Dilatancy

N, none—No visible change in the specimen.

S, slow—Water appears slowly on the surface of the specimen during shaking and does not disappear or disappears slowly upon squeezing.

R, rapid—Water appears quickly on the surface of the specimen during shaking and disappears quickly upon squeezing.

Toughness

L, low—Only slight pressure is required to roll the thread near the plastic limit. The thread and the lump are weak and soft.

M, medium—Medium pressure is required to roll the thread to near the plastic limit. The thread and the lump have medium stiffness.

H, high—Considerable pressure is required to roll the thread near the plastic limit. The thread and the lump have very high stiffness.

Plasticity

N, nonplastic—A 3-millimeter thread cannot be rolled at any water content.

L, low—The thread can barely be rolled and the lump cannot be formed when drier than the plastic limit.

M, medium—The thread is easy to roll and not much time is required to reach the plastic limit. The thread cannot be rerolled after reaching the plastic limit. The lump crumbles when drier than the plastic limit.

H, high—It takes considerable time rolling and kneading to reach the plastic limit. The thread can be rerolled several times after reaching the plastic limit. The lump can be formed without crumbling when drier than the plastic limit.

Unified Class (Unified Soil Classification System)

ML, silt

CL, clay

MH, silt of high plasticity, elastic silt

Dip Angle

V, vertical

SV, subvertical

M, medium

SH, subhorizontal

H, horizontal

Appendix 1A

REGOLITH LOG SHEET
PROJECT: ALLISON WOODS
BORING ID: CH-1
LOGGED BY: PIPPIN
BEGIN DATE: 5/3/2005
END DATE: 5/13/2005
(ft bls, feet below land surface)

DRILLING METHOD: Wireline coring / Split-spoon
CORE DIAMETER: 2.5"
LATITUDE: 35.90841937
LONGITUDE: -80.823227887
LAND SURFACE ELEVATION: 899.71'
Color descriptions referenced to Munsell soil color charts.

Interval (ft bls)	Recovery	Grain size	Dry/wet	Color	Dry strength	Dilantancy	Plasticity	Unified class	Description	Groundwater zone
0–5	1'	F	D	2.5YR 4/6 RED		N	M	MH	Humic material to 1"; compacted during recovery; red SANDY SILT.	REGOLITH (residuum)
5–8	0'								No recovery.	REGOLITH (residuum)
8–13	5'	F	D	2.5YR 4/6 RED TO 2.5YR 4/1 GRAYISH RED	L	N	N	MH TO ML	Roots to 9'; then, darker in color; MnO stains; relict foliation; kaolonite pods 0–3 cm; coarse kyanite granules; fine MICACEOUS SILT.	REGOLITH (residuum)
13–18	3'	F	D	2.5YR 4/1 GRAYISH RED	L	N	N	ML	Fine MICACEOUS SILT; No recovery from 13' to 15'; relict foliations at 15'–18'; MnO stains parallel & perpendicular to foliation; at 15.5' is a 6" quartz & kaolinite band followed by 12" of kyanite sand adjacent to relict foliations of gneiss & schist.	REGOLITH (residuum)
18–23	5'	F	D	2.5YR GRAYISH RED TO 7.5YR 5/8 BROWN	N to VH	S	N	ML	Grayish red to brown MICACEOUS to NONMICACEOUS SILT; at 21', very hard 2' zone; then, returns to silt; frequent black MnO spots.	REGOLITH (residuum)
23–28	5'	F	D	7.5 YR 5/8 BROWN	L TO VH	S	N	ML	Brown MICACEOUS SILT; friable at 23'.	REGOLITH (residuum)
28–33	5'	F	D	7.5 YR 5/8 STRONG BROWN	L	S	N	ML	Strong brown MICACEOUS SILT; fine grained; many MnO stains parallel to relict foliation.	REGOLITH (residuum)
33–34	1'	F	D	7.5 YR 5/8 STRONG BROWN	L	S	N	ML	Strong brown MICACEOUS SILT; fine grained; several MnO stains parallel to relict foliation.	REGOLITH (residuum)
34–39	1'	F	D	7.5 YR 5/8 STRONG BROWN	L	S	N	ML	Strong brown MICACEOUS SILT; fine grained; several MnO stains parallel to relict foliation.	REGOLITH (residuum)
39–44	2'	F	D	2.5YR 5/4 OLIVE BROWN	L	N	N	ML	Olive brown MICACEOUS SILT; relict foliations with low dip angle; relict garnets altered to MnO nodules.	REGOLITH (residuum)
44–49	20"	F	D	2.5YR 5/4 OLIVE BROWN	L	N	N	ML	Olive brown MICACEOUS SILT; relict foliations with low dip angle; relict garnets altered to MnO nodules.	REGOLITH (residuum)
49–54	16"	F	D	2.5YR 5/4 OLIVE BROWN	L	N	N	ML	At 49' to 49.5', hard rock (biotite hornblende gneiss) with subvertical fractures; below, MICACEOUS SILT similar to 44' to 49' section.	REGOLITH (residuum)
54–59	5'	F	D	2.5YR 5/4 OLIVE BROWN	L	N	N	ML	MICACEOUS SILT becoming PARTIALLY WEATHERED ROCK, which is brown in color with preserved foliation & phenocrysts; at 58.5', 2" of competant biotite gneiss; then, returns to partially weathered rock.	TRANSITION ZONE

<table>
<tr><td colspan="9" align="center">Appendix 1A—Continued</td></tr>
<tr>
<td colspan="5">
BEDROCK LOG SHEET
PROJECT: ALLISON WOODS
BORING ID: CH-1
LOGGED BY: PIPPIN
BEGIN DATE: 05/03/2005
END DATE: 05/13/2005
</td>
<td colspan="4">
DRILLING METHOD: WIRELINE CORING
CORE DIAMETER: 2.5"
</td>
</tr>
</table>

		Lithologic description		Fracture info				
Interval	Recovery	Description		# An-nealed	# Open	H2O Bearing	Minerals	Groundwater zone
59–64	5'	PARTIALLY WEATHERED ROCK from 59–60'; then, BIOTITE GARNET SCHIST to HORN-BLENDE GARNET SCHIST; mineral dissolution apparent at 60–61'.	H		5	62.0		TRANSITION ZONE
			SH		1	63.0		
			M			63.5		
			SV					
			V					
64–65	1'	BIOTITE GARNET SCHIST to HORNBLENDE GARNET SCHIST; 4" QUARTZ BIOTITE ZONE; several open fractures, parallel to foliation.	H		8	64.0		TRANSITION ZONE
			SH			to		
			M			65.0		
			SV					
			V					
65–70	2' 4"	HORNBLENDE SCHIST becomes more garnet rich at 68; quartz vein at 66'; 68–70', HORNBLENDE GARNET SCHIST; fracture frequency decreases.	H		13	65.0		TRANSITION ZONE
			SH			to		
			M		1	68.0		
			SV					
			V					
70–75	5'	BIOTITE SCHIST from 70–71'; then, HORN-BLENDE SCHIST dominates with interlayers of BIOTITE SCHIST.	H		6	71.0	FeO	BEDROCK
			SH			to		
			M			74.0		
			SV		1			
			V			75.0		
75–80	5'	Grain size decreases to fine grained; more stretched out porphyroblasts; alternates between BIOTITE HORNBLENDE SCHIST and BIOTITE SCHIST; quartz bands are boudins or veins.	H		2	75.0		BEDROCK
			SH			to		
			M			76.0		
			SV		1			
			V					
80–85	5'	Alternates between BIOTITE HORNBLENDE SCHIST and BIOTITE SCHIST; 1" thick leu-cocratic zone at 80'; mostly fine grained to 84'; then, hornblende schist with coarse grains, garnet increases; slickensides parallel to foliation.	H		4	82.0		BEDROCK
			SH		1	to		
			M			83.0		
			SV			83.8		
			V					
85–90	5'	HORNBLENDE SCHIST; At 86', rock becomes finer grained with decreasing hornblende & increasing quartz-feldspar; at 87', QUARTZO-FELDSPATHIC GNEISS; at 89, HORNBLENDE BIOTITE gneiss.	H		6			BEDROCK
			SH					
			M			89.0		
			SV			to		
			V			90.0		
90–95	5'	BIOTITE GNEISS with deformed quartz augens; no fractures.	H					BEDROCK
			SH					
			M					
			SV					
			V					
95–100	5'	BIOTITE GNEISS; Increasing hornblende and garnet; becomes AMPHIBOLITE GNEISS at 96'.	H		1			BEDROCK
			SH			96.5		
			M					
			SV					
			V					

	Appendix 1B

REGOLITH LOG SHEET
PROJECT: ALLISON WOODS
BORING ID: CH-2
LOGGED BY: PIPPIN
BEGIN DATE: 04/06/2005
END DATE: 04/28/2005
(ft bls, feet below land surface)

DRILLING METHOD: Wireline coring
CORE DIAMETER: 2.5"
LATITUDE: 35.907858892
LONGITUDE: -80.825127447
LAND SURFACE ELEVATION: 870.58'
Color descriptions referenced to Munsell soil color charts

Interval (ft bls)	Recovery	Grain size	Dry/wet	Color	Dry strength	Dilan-tancy	Plas-ticity	Uni-fied class	Description	Groundwater zone
0–5	3'	F	D	2.5YR 5/8 RED	M	N	M	CL	Red, CLAYEY SILT with sand to COARSE SAND composed of quartz & kyanite	REGOLITH (residuum)
5–10	2'	F TO M	M	10 YR 4/4 YELLOWISH BROWN	N	S	N	MH	Yellowish brown SILT with mica from 5' to 6'; then, medium grained well foliated saprolite; abundant MnO stains at 6'; a white quartz to feld-spar clay zone 2' wide.	REGOLITH (residuum)
10–15	10"	M	M TO W	5 YR 4/2 DARK REDDISH GRAY			N	SW	Medium grained SAND composed of kyanite blades and mica; slight cohesiveness; no clay content.	REGOLITH (residuum)
15–20	2"	F	M	10 YR 4/4 YELLOWISH BROWN	N	S	M	MH	Yellowsh brown SILT with clay; quartz & feldspar alter to clay with MICACEOUS SILT.	REGOLITH (residuum)
20–25	0'								No recovery	REGOLITH (residuum)
25–30	2"	F	M	10 YR 4/4 YELLOWISH BROWN		S	M	MH	Yellowsh brown SILT with clay; quartz & feldspar alter to clay with MICACEOUS SILT.	REGOLITH (residuum)
30–35	11"	F	W	10 YR 4/4 YELLOWISH BROWN		S	M	MH	Yellowsh brown SILT with sand; little clay.	REGOLITH (residuum)
35–37.5	20"	F	W	10 YR 4/2 DARK GRAYISH BROWN		S	M	MH	Dark grayish brown MICACEOUS SILT; 2' zone of weathered quartz & feldspar followed by 6" of orange-red silt with MnO stains.	REGOLITH (residuum)
37.5–40	2.5'	F	W	10 YR 4/2 DARK GRAYISH BROWN		R	N	ML	Dark grayish brown MICACEOUS SILT, mottled with brown oxide partches.	REGOLITH (residuum)
40–42.5	20"	F	W	10 YR 4/2 DARK GRAYISH BROWN		S	L	ML	Dark grayish brown MICACEOUS SILT with minor clay & sand; bio-tite altered to vermiculite	REGOLITH (residuum)
42.5–45	21"	F	W	10 YR 4/2 DARK GRAYISH BROWN		S	L	ML	Dark grayish brown MICACEOUS SILT with minor clay & sand; bio-tite altered to vermiculite	REGOLITH (residuum)
45–48	35"	F		7.5 YR 4/3 BROWN		N	N	ML	Brown SILT with sand; relict composi-tional banding preserved; FeO & MnO stains; 3" pegmatite zone at 47'.	REGOLITH (residuum)
48–50	2'	F		7.5 YR 4/3 BROWN		N	N	ML	Brown SILT with sand; relict composi-tional banding preserved; FeO & MnO stains.	REGOLITH (residuum)
50–53	3'	F TO M		7.5 YR 4/3 BROWN		N	N	ML	Brown SILT and SAND; becomes more saprolitic; hard & soft inter-vals at 0.5" to 1" intervals.	REGOLITH (residuum)
53–55	2'	F TO M		7.5 YR 4/3 BROWN		N	N	ML	Brown SILT and SAND; becomes more saprolitic; 6" intervals of garnet-biotite schist.	REGOLITH (residuum)

Appendix 1B—Continued		

BEDROCK LOG SHEET
PROJECT: ALLISON WOODS
BORING ID: CH-2
LOGGED BY: PIPPIN
BEGIN DATE: 04/06/2005
END DATE: 04/28/2005

DRILLING METHOD: Wireline Coring
CORE DIAMETER: 2.5"

		Lithologic description		Fracture info				
Interval	Recovery	Description		# Annealed	# Open	H2O Bearing	Minerals	Groundwater zone
55–60	5'	Saprolitic BIOTITE GARNET SCHIST; several horizonatal fractures; two high anagle fractures; FeO on fractures; competent rock at 60'.	H		16	56.0	BIOTITE GARNET HORNBL QUARTZ EPIDOTE FEO	TRANSITION ZONE
			SH			to		
			M			60.0		
			SV		2			
			V					
60–65	2'	First 6" of recovered core is highly weathered rock; with FeO stains; Saprolitic biotite garnet SCHIST; last 6" is solid rock; quartz & feldspar phenocrysts show minor stretches & left lateral rotations; weak gneissic banding.	H		2	60.5	BIOTITE GARNET QUARTZ FELDSPAR FeO PYRITE	TRANSITION ZONE
			SH					
			M					
			SV					
			V					
65–70	5'	65–66', SCHIST; then, 8" of micaceous sand & silt with no clay; highly weathered rock; at 66.5', 4" quartz vein parallel to foliation; at 67', shear zone evidenced by well aligned biotite and stretched quartz & feldspar; at 68', second 6" of sheared zone, very coarse grained; at 68.5', weakly foliated AMPHIBOLITE GNEISS.	H		10	65.0	QUARTZ FELDSPAR BIOTITE	TRANSITION ZONE
			SH		2	to		
			M		3	69.0		
			SV					
			V					
70–75	5'	70–71' weakly foliated AMPHIBOLITE GNEISS; 71–74', biotite garnet gneiss; garnet, up to 20% between 71 and 72.5', then decreases; 73.5' to 75', amphibolite with weak to moderate foliation; shear zone at 74–74.5'.	H		4	70.5	BIOTITE GARNET HORNBL	BEDROCK
			SH			73.0		
			M			to		
			SV			74.0		
			V	2				
75–80	5'	75–77.5', fine grained AMPHIBOLITE GNEISS with migmatitic zone at 75.5'; abundant phenocrysts of feldspars with tails showing right lateral shear component; 78–80', BIOTITE GNEISS dominates; at 79', a 2" thick granitic band (dike?), parallel to foliation, foliation moderately dipping at <30.	H		1	75.5	FELDSPAR BIOTITE HORNBL	BEDROCK
			SH			77.5		
			M			80.0		
			SV					
			V	4				
80–85	5'	Alternating BIOTITE and AMPHIBOLITE GNEISS; coarse grained migmatitic zone at 80.7'; high fracture density; fractures parallel to foliation in amphibolite gneiss; a zone of migmatite zone at 83 to 84', where grain boundaries show evidence of dissolution; at 84', foliation dip increases followed by zone of greater weathering.	H		19			BEDROCK
			SH					
			M			82.0		
			SV	1		to		
			V			85.0		
85–90	56"	Migmatitic zone or granitic dike at 85 to 85.5'; then, BIOTITE and AMPHIBOLITE GNEISS; at 87', small granitic zone, acting as water-bearing; 87–90', AUGEN GNEISS, consisting of biotite, feldspar, quartz with phenocrysts of quartz (augen), minor garnet, fractures at 85' and 87'.	H		9	85.5	BIOTITE HORNBL QUARTZ FELDSPAR GARNET	BEDROCK
			SH			87.0		
			M			to		
			SV			88.0		
			V			89.2		
90–95	5'	AUGEN GNEISS as above; intermittent biotite gneiss bands; water-bearing fractures at 90'10", 92'6", 94'8", 95'2"; foliation shallow(<20), minor garnet.	H		4	90.0	QUARTZ FELDSPAR BIOTITE GARNET	BEDROCK
			SH			90.8		
			M			92.5		
			SV			94.7		
			V					

Appendix 1B—Continued							
BEDROCK LOG SHEET PROJECT: ALLISON WOODS BORING ID: CH-2 LOGGED BY: PIPPIN BEGIN DATE: 04/06/2005 END DATE: 04/28/2005				DRILLING METHOD: Wireline Coring CORE DIAMETER: 2.5"			

		Lithologic description		Fracture info				
Interval	Recov-ery	Description		# An-nealed	# Open	H2O Bearing	Minerals	Groundwater zone
95–100	5'	AUGEN GNEISS; intermittent biotite gneiss bands	H		9	95.8	QUARTZ FELDSPAR BIOTITE GARNET	BEDROCK
			SH			to		
			M			97.0		
			SV		1	98.2		
			V					
100–105	5'	AUGEN GNEISS	H			100.0	QUARTZ FELDSPAR BIOTITE GARNET	BEDROCK
			SH					
			M					
			SV	1				
			V					
105–110		AUGEN GNEISS	H		2	105.0	QUARTZ FELDSPAR BIOTITE GARNET	BEDROCK
			SH			108.0		
			M			109.0		
			SV					
			V	1				
110–115	5'	AUGEN GNEISS	H				QUARTZ FELDSPAR BIOTITE GARNET	BEDROCK
			SH					
			M	1				
			SV					
			V	2				
115–120	5'	AUGEN GNEISS; 118–120', leucocratic zones	H				QUARTZ FELDSPAR BIOTITE GARNET	BEDROCK
			SH					
			M					
			SV					
			V	1				
120–125		AUGEN GNEISS; becomes more garnetiferous phe-nocrysts; at 123.5–125', thick leucocratic zone.	H				QUARTZ FELDSPAR BIOTITE GARNET EPIDOTE	BEDROCK
			SH					
			M	1				
			SV					
			V	1				
125–130		Hornblende dominated GNEISS; garnets more abun-dant.	H				HORNBL GARNET EPIDOTE	BEDROCK
			SH					
			M					
			SV					
			V	1				
130–135		HORNBLENDE BIOTITE GNEISS; less banding	H				HORNBL BIOTITE	BEDROCK
			SH					
			M					
			SV					
			V					
135–140		HORNBLENDE BIOTITE GNEISS	H				HORNBL BIOTITE	BEDROCK
			SH					
			M					
			SV		4			
			V					

Appendix 1B—Continued							
BEDROCK LOG SHEET PROJECT: ALLISON WOODS BORING ID: CH-2 LOGGED BY: PIPPIN BEGIN DATE: 04/06/2005 END DATE: 04/28/2005			DRILLING METHOD: Wireline Coring CORE DIAMETER: 2.5"				

		Lithologic description		Fracture info				
Interval	Recov-ery	Description		# An-nealed	# Open	H20 Bearing	Minerals	Groundwater zone
140–145		HORNBLENDE BIOTITE GNEISS; becomes more biotite rich at 144'.	H				HORNBL BIOTITE	BEDROCK
			SH					
			M					
			SV					
			V					
145–150		BITOTE GNEISS with thick leucocratic zones	H		2	2.0	BIOTITE PYRITE	BEDROCK
			SH		1	1.0		
			M	1				
			SV					
			V	1				
150–155	5'	BITOTE GNEISS with thick leucocratic zones	H		3	3.0	BIOTITE	BEDROCK
			SH					
			M					
			SV					
			V	2				
155–160	5'	BITOTE GNEISS; less felsic zones; foliation dip angle is shallow (<15); quartz annealed fracture dip ~75 at 156'.	H		1		BIOTITE	BEDROCK
			SH					
			M					
			SV	1				
			V					
160–165	5'	BIOTITE GNEISS; an annealed fracture with bluish color.	H				BIOTITE	BEDROCK
			SH					
			M					
			SV	1				
			V					
165–170	5'	BIOTITE GNEISS	H				BIOTITE	BEDROCK
			SH					
			M					
			SV					
			V					
170–175	5'	BIOTITE GNEISS	H				BIOTITE	BEDROCK
			SH					
			M					
			SV					
			V					
175–180	5'	BIOTITE GNEISS; quartz annealed vein	H				BIOTITE	BEDROCK
			SH					
			M					
			SV					
			V	1				
180–185	5'	BIOTITE GNEISS	H		1	182.1	BIOTITE	BEDROCK
			SH					
			M					
			SV					
			V					

Appendix 1B—Continued								
BEDROCK LOG SHEET PROJECT: ALLISON WOODS BORING ID: CH-2 LOGGED BY: PIPPIN BEGIN DATE: 04/06/2005 END DATE: 04/28/2005				DRILLING METHOD: Wireline Coring CORE DIAMETER: 2.5"				
		Lithologic description		Fracture info				
Interval	Recov-ery	Description		# An-nealed	# Open	H2O Bearing	Minerals	Groundwater zone
185–190	5'	BIOTITE GNEISS	H				BIOTITE	BEDROCK
			SH					
			M					
			SV					
			V					
190–195	5'	HORNBLENDE GARNET BIOTITE GNEISS; QUARTZ EPIDOTE ZONE between 190'8"–192'2" with thin layers of biotite grains; between 192'2" to 194'10" hetrogeneous zone of qtz, epi, bio, hornbl, and actinolite (?); mechanical fractures between 190 and 192'.	H		1	192.7	HORNBL GARNET BIOTITE QUARTZ EPIDOTE	BEDROCK
			SH					
			M					
			SV					
			V					
195–200	5'	HORNBLENDE GARNET BIOTITE GNEISS; at 195'7"–198'4", QUARTZ EPIDOTE zone.	H		1	1.0	HORNBL GARNET BIOTITE QUARTZ FELDSPAR EPIDOTE	BEDROCK
			SH					
			M					
			SV					
			V					

Appendix 1C										
REGOLITH LOG SHEET PROJECT: ALLISON WOODS BORING ID: CH-3 LOGGED BY: PIPPIN BEGIN DATE: 05/24/2005 END DATE: 5/25/2005 (ft bls, feet below land surface)						DRILLING METHOD: Split-spoon CORE DIAMETER: 2.5" LATITUDE: 35.90637611 LONGITUDE: -80.825343143 LAND SURFACE ELEVATION: 851.02' Color descriptions referenced to Munsell soil color charts.				

Interval (ft bls)	Re-covery	Grain size	Dry/wet	Color	Dry strength	Dilan-tancy	Plastic-ity	Unified class	Description	Groundwater zone
0–3	3'	F	M	7.5YR 4/6 STRONG BROWN	M	N	M	SC	Grayish brown clayey SAND	REGOLITH (residuum)
3–8	5'	F	M	10YR 8/3 PALE BROWN	N	R	N	SC TO MH	Pale brown SANDY CLAY turning to brownish MICACEOUS SILT.	REGOLITH (residuum)
8–13	5'	F	M	2.5YR 4/1 DARK REDDISH GRAY	N	R	N	MH	QUARTZ VEIN at 8'–10'; lots of Fe stains; 10'–13', MICACEOUS SILT.	REGOLITH (residuum)
13–18	5'	F	M	2.5YR 4/1 DARK REDDISH GRAY	N	R	N	MH TO SM	Between 13'–15', two zones (4" each) of quartz & feldspar sand; then, MICACEOUS SILT.	REGOLITH (residuum)
18–23	5'	F	M	10YR 4/4 DARK YEL-LOWISH BROWN	N	R	N	SM	MICACEOUS SILT with sand; 1" QUARTZ VEIN at 19'.	REGOLITH (residuum)
23–25	6"	F	M	10YR 4/4 DARK YEL-LOWISH BROWN		R	N	SM	Brown MICACEOUS SILTY SAND with amphibole granules; PARTIALLY WEATHERED ROCK.	TRANSITION ZONE
25–28	18"	M	M	10YR 4/4 DARK YEL-LOWISH BROWN		R	N	SM	Brown MICACEOUS SILTY SAND; turning to PARTIALLY WEATHERED ROCK at 28' and COMPETENT ROCK at 28.5'.	TRANSITION ZONE

Appendix 1C—Continued								
BEDROCK LOG SHEET PROJECT: ALLISON WOODS BORING ID: CH-3 LOGGED BY: PIPPIN BEGIN DATE: 05/24/2005 END DATE: 5/25/2005					DRILLING METHOD: WIRELINE CORING CORE DIAMETER: 2.5"			

Interval	Recov-ery	Description		# An-nealed	# Open	H2O bear-ing	Minerals	Groundwater zone
28–30	2'	Fine grained BIOTITE HORNBLENDE GNEISS.	H				BIOTITE HORNBL	TRANSITION ZONE
			SH					
			M					
			SV					
			V					
30–35	5'	Fine to medium grained AMPHIBOLITE GNEISS.	H		1		HORNBL	BEDROCK
			SH					
			M					
			SV			34.5		
			V					
35–40	5'	AMPHIBOLITE GNEISS to 38'; then, BIOTITE GNEISS.	H				HORNBL BIOTITE	BEDROCK
			SH					
			M					
			SV					
			V					
40–45	5'	BIOTITE GNEISS and AMPHIBOLITE GNEISS.	H				BIOTITE HORNBL	BEDROCK
			SH					
			M					
			SV					
			V					
45–50	5'	AMPHIBOLITE GNEISS and BIOTITE GNEISS.	H				BIOTITE HORNBL	BEDROCK
			SH					
			M					
			SV					
			V					
50–55	5'	BIOTITE GNEISS to 52.5'; then, AMPHIBOLITE GNEISS; leucocratic zone.	H				BIOTITE HORNBL	BEDROCK
			SH					
			M					
			SV					
			V					
55–60	5'	Leucocratic zone to 56'; BIOTITE HORNBLENDE GARNET GNEISS.	H		3	55.5	BIOTITE HORNBL GARNET	BEDROCK
			SH			to		
			M			56.0		
			SV					
			V					

Appendix 1C—Continued							
BEDROCK LOG SHEET PROJECT: ALLISON WOODS BORING ID: CH-3 LOGGED BY: PIPPIN BEGIN DATE: 05/24/2005 END DATE: 5/25/2005				DRILLING METHOD: WIRELINE CORING CORE DIAMETER: 2.5"			

		Lithologic description		Fracture info				
Interval	Recovery	Description		# Annealed	# Open	H2O bearing	Minerals	Groundwater zone
60–65	5'	BIOTITE HORNBLENDE GARNET GNEISS to 62'; then, AMPHIBOLITE GNEISS.	H		1	63.5	BIOTITE HORNBL GARNET	BEDROCK
			SH					
			M					
			SV					
			V					
65–70	5'	AMPHIBOLITE GNEISS	H		1	67.0	BIOTITE HORNBL	BEDROCK
			SH					
			M					
			SV					
			V					
70–75	5'	AMPHIBOLITE GNEISS and BIOTITE HORN-BLENDE GARNET GNEISS.	H				BIOTITE HORNBL	BEDROCK
			SH					
			M					
			SV					
			V					

									Appendix 1D	

REGOLITH LOG SHEET
PROJECT: ALLISON WOODS
BORING ID: CH-4
LOGGED BY: PIPPIN
BEGIN DATE: 05/24/2005
END DATE: 05/27/2005
(ft bls, feet below land surface)

DRILLING METHOD: Split-spoon
CORE DIAMETER: 2.5"
LATITUDE: 35.907739039
LONGITUDE: -80.82691214
LAND SURFACE ELEVATION: 836.26'
Color descriptions referenced to Munsell soil color charts.

Interval (ft bls)	Recov-ery	Grain size	Dry/wet	Color	Dry strength	Dilan-tancy	Plas-ticity	Unified class	Description	Groundwater zone
0–3	3'	F TO C	M	7.5 YR 5/8 STRONG BROWN	L	N	L	ML	Brown root-bearing SANDY SILT to 4"; 4" to 3', strong brown sandy silt; at 2' to 3', large quartz & amphibolite clasts and many kyanite blades	REGOLITH (residuum)
3–8	5'	F TO C	M	7.5 YR 5/8 STRONG BROWN	L	N	N	ML TO SM	Brown to grayish brown SANDY SILT to SILTY SAND with very coarse sand/pebble zone at 4' to 6'; below sharp contact with amphibolite/ biotite/garnet schist saprolite with relict foliation and relict garnet pophyroblasts.	REGOLITH (residuum)
8–13	5'	F	M	10 YR 4/2 DARK GRAYISH BROWN	L	R	N	SM TO ML	Brown SANDY SILT to SILTY SAND; relict gneiss alternating bands of mica-rich soils and harder quart-feldspar zones; bottom 6", coarse grained quartz & feldspar.	REGOLITH (residuum)
13–18	5'	F	M	GRAY	N	R	N	MH	Gray MICACEOUS SILT.	REGOLITH (residuum)
18–23	5'	F	M	GRAY	N	R	N	MH TO SM	Gray MICACEOUS SILT to SANDY CLAY.	REGOLITH (residuum)
23–28	5'	F	M	GRAY	L	R	N	MH	Gray MICACEOUS SILT with zones of PARTIALLY WEATHERED ROCK.	TRANSI-TION ZONE
28–30	2'	F	M	GRAY	L	R	N	MH	Gray MICACEOUS SILT with zones of PARTIALLY WEATHERED ROCK.	TRANSI-TION ZONE

Appendix 1D—Continued		

BEDROCK LOG SHEET
PROJECT: ALLISON WOODS
BORING ID: CH-4
LOGGED BY: PIPPIN
BEGIN DATE: 05/24/2005
END DATE: 05/27/2005

DRILLING METHOD: Wireline Coring
CORE DIAMETER: 2.5"

		Lithologic description		Fracture info				
Interval	Recov-ery	Description		# An-nealed	# Open	H2O bear-ing	Minerals	Groundwater zone
30–35	5'	At 30–31', white coarse grained quartz feldspar anatomizing fabric (< 2 cm); from 31', grayish garnet (up to 1 cm diameter) KYANITE BIOTITE SCHIST with stretch porpyroblasts of feldspar.	H		7	32.5	BIOTITE	TRANSITION ZONE
			SH					
			M		1	33.5		
			SV			to		
			V			35.0		
35–40	5'	KYANITE SCHIST; garnets smaller (3–4 mm); gneissic banding; highly fractured interval at 35–36'.	H		8	35.0	KYANITE	TRANSITION ZONE
			SH			to		
			M		1	37.0		
			SV					
			V					
40–45	5'	At 40–43', KYANITE BIOTITE GARNET GNEISS with quartz-feldspar bands; at 43–45', coarse grained QUARTZ-FELDSPAR ZONE.	H		2		KYANITE BIOTITE GARNET QUARTZ FELD-SPAR	BEDROCK
			SH			42.5		
			M			43.0		
			SV					
			V					
45–50	5'	At 45–47', coarse grained QUARTZ-FELDSPAR ZONE; 47–48', KYANITE-GARNET SCHIST; 49–49.25' QUARTZ-FELDSPAR ZONE; 49.25–50', KYANITE SCHIST.	H		1		KYANITE BIOTITE GARNET QUARTZ FELD-SPAR	BEDROCK
			SH					
			M					
			SV			48.0		
			V					
50–55	5'	KYANITE BIOTITE GARNET GNEISS with quartz-feldspar bands; no observed fractures.	H				KYANITE BIOTITE GARNET QUARTZ FELD-SPAR	BEDROCK
			SH					
			M					
			SV					
			V					
55–60	5'	KYANITE GARNET BIOTITE SCHIST with quartz-feldspar bands; at 58–60', kyanite absent, coarse grained QUARTZ-FELDSPAR ZONE with biotite-rich gneissic bands.	H		1		KYANITE BIOTITE GARNET QUARTZ FELD-SPAR	BEDROCK
			SH					
			M					
			SV					
			V					
60–65	5'	Coarse grained QUARTZ-FELDSPAR ZONE from 60–62'; then, alternating biotite-rich GNEISS and amphibolite-rich gneiss; water-bearing fractures at 65'.	H		3		BIOTITE QUARTZ FELD-SPAR	BEDROCK
			SH					
			M					
			SV			64.5		
			V					
65–70	5'	BITOTITE GNEISS; water bearing at 66'; from 67–70', fine to medium grained quartz, biotite, feldspar, garnet, pyroxene, LEUCOCRATIC GNEISS; no fractures.	H		1		BIOTITE QUARTZ FELD-SPAR GARNET PYX	BEDROCK
			SH			66.0		
			M					
			SV					
			V					

<table>
<tr><td colspan="9" align="center">Appendix 1D—Continued</td></tr>
<tr><td colspan="5">BEDROCK LOG SHEET
PROJECT: ALLISON WOODS
BORING ID: CH-4
LOGGED BY: PIPPIN
BEGIN DATE: 05/24/2005
END DATE: 05/27/2005</td><td colspan="4">DRILLING METHOD: Wireline Coring
CORE DIAMETER: 2.5"</td></tr>
</table>

		Lithologic description		Fracture info				
Interval	Recovery	Description		# Annealed	# Open	H2O bearing	Minerals	Groundwater zone
70–75	5'	LEUCOCRATIC GNEISS from 70–73'; then, BIOTITE GNEISS alternating with AMPHIBOLITE GNEISS; garnets present.	H		4	72.5	BIOTITE GARNET	BEDROCK
			SH			to		
			M			74.0		
			SV	1				
			V					
75–80	5'	BIOTITE GNEISS alternating with AMPHIBOLITE GNEISS.	H				BIOTITE GARNET	BEDROCK
			SH					
			M					
			SV					
			V					
80–85	5'	AMPHIBOLOITE GNEISS; local zone of anatomizing feldspar and biotite; at 85', garnets become abundant.	H		1		BIOTITE GARNET	BEDROCK
			SH					
			M					
			SV					
			V					
85–90	5'	AMPHIBOLITE GNEISS; at 85–87', garnets abundant.	H				BIOTITE GARNET	BEDROCK
			SH					
			M					
			SV					
			V					
90–95	5'	AMPHIBOLITE GNEISS to BIOTITE GNEISS; feldspar and biotite more anatomizing from 90.5–91.5'; one (3 cm) large porphyroblast of feldspar.	H				BIOTITE GARNET FELDSPAR	BEDROCK
			SH					
			M					
			SV					
			V					
95–100	5'	AMPHIBOLITE GNEISS to BIOTITE GNEISS; at 95'; 1 cm garnet porphyroblasts; at 97–99', feldspar & biotite zone; grades into biotite gneiss with thin amphibolite bands from 99 to 100'.	H				BIOTITE GARNET FELDSPAR	BEDROCK
			SH					
			M					
			SV					
			V					

Appendix 2. Analytical water-quality results from samples collected in November 2006 and July 2007 at the Allison Woods research station, Iredell County, North Carolina.

[mg/L, milligrams per liter; µS/cm, microsiemens per centimeter at 25 degrees Celsius; C, degrees Celsius; $CaCO_3$, calcium carbonate; E, estimated; <, less than; µg/L, micrograms per liter; N, Nitrogen]

Well number	Station number	Sample date	Oxygen, dissolved (mg/L)	pH field (standard units)	Specific conductance (µS/cm)	Water temperature (°C)	Calcium, dissolved (mg/L)	Magnesium, dissolved (mg/L)	Potassium, dissolved (mg/L)	Sodium, dissolved (mg/L)	Alkalinity, dissolved, field (mg/L as $CaCO_3$)	Bromide, dissolved (mg/L)
MW-1I	355429080492302	11-28-06	4.7	6.0	114	15.3	6.87	2.69	3.97	8.67	40	E 0.01
		07-09-07	*	6.3	89	16.1	6.43	2.57	2.95	6.32	33	E 0.01
MW-1D	355429080492303	11-28-06	0.2	*	*	16.8	*	*	*	*	*	*
		07-09-07	*	*	*	17.5	*	*	*	*	*	*
CH-1	355429080492304	11-28-06	3.9	6.8	157	15.1	15.5	4.36	3.53	5.68	59	<0.02
MW-2S	355428080493001	11-28-06	6.0	5.3	20	14.8	0.44	0.60	1.12	1.09	5	E 0.01
		07-10-07	9.4	5.2	16	14.8	0.42	0.61	1.18	0.59	4	E 0.01
MW-2I	355428080493002	11-28-06	1.7	6.6	163	15.6	19.8	3.81	5.43	5.35	67	E 0.02
		07-10-07	1.9	7.0	152	16.2	17.2	3.03	5.57	4.30	64	E 0.01
MW-2D	355428080493003	11-28-06	0.7	7.6	153	16.7	17.3	4.07	4.86	4.43	65	E 0.01
		07-09-07	2.2	7.2	139	15.4	14.2	3.57	4.51	4.09	57	*
MW-3S	355422080493101	11-29-06	3.1	5.3	53	17.0	3.59	2.23	1.07	1.83	17	E 0.01
		07-11-07	2.2	5.2	58	14.4	3.96	2.47	1.14	1.86	16	<0.02
MW-3I	355422080493102	11-29-06	5.1	6.0	89	14.3	5.84	2.57	3.48	3.93	24	E 0.02
		07-11-07	5.9	5.8	85	13.9	6.49	2.62	2.56	3.87	23	<0.02
MW-3D	355422080493103	11-29-06	0.5	*	*	15.3	*	*	*	*	*	*
		07-10-07	0.4	*	*	18.5	*	*	*	*	*	*
MW-4S	355427080493701	11-29-06	2.6	4.8	25	15.5	0.73	0.86	0.77	1.07	8	E 0.01
		07-10-07	8.4	5.2	20	14.6	0.73	0.88	0.76	1.07	6	<0.02
MW-4I	355427080493702	11-29-06	7.2	6.1	71	14.3	6.91	2.03	1.49	3.35	33	E 0.01
		07-10-07	10.6	6.3	70	14.4	6.79	2.06	1.57	3.76	30	E 0.01
MW-4D	355427080493703	11-29-06	0.1	*	*	16.3	*	*	*	*	*	*
		07-10-07	0.3	*	*	15.9	*	*	*	*	*	*
STREAM	02117495	07-11-07	7.2	6.1	60	17.4	4.54	2.30	1.24	2.95	21	<0.02

* Not analyzed or not reported due to suspected grout contamination.

Appendix 2. Analytical water-quality results from samples collected in November 2006 and July 2007 at the Allison Woods research station, Iredell County, North Carolina.—Continued

[mg/L, milligrams per liter; µS/cm, microsiemens per centimeter at 25 degrees Celsius; C, degrees Celsius; CaCO$_3$, calcium carbonate; E, estimated; <, less than; µg/L, micrograms per liter; N, Nitrogen]

Well number	Station number	Sample date	Chloride, dissolved (mg/L)	Fluoride, dissolved (mg/L)	Silica, dissolved (mg/L)	Sulfate, dissolved (mg/L)	Total dissolved solids, residue at 180 °C (mg/L)	Ammonia, dissolved (mg/L as N)	Nitrate plus nitrite, dissolved (mg/L as N)	Nitrite, dissolved (mg/L as N)	Total nitrogen (nitrate + nitrite + ammonia + organic-N), dissolved (mg/L)	Phosphorus, ortho, dissolved (mg/L)
MW-1I	355429080492302	11-28-06	2.82	<0.1	15.2	7.85	67	<0.02	0.22	0.003	0.25	0.008
		07-09-07	2.41	E 0.06	15.5	5.87	63	<0.02	0.17	<0.002	0.17	0.009
MW-1D	355429080492303	11-28-06	*	*	*	*	*	<0.02	<0.06	<0.002	<0.06	0.009
		07-09-07	*	*	*	*	*	<0.02	<0.06	<0.002	<0.06	0.011
CH-1	355429080492304	11-28-06	2.33	E 0.05	27.5	9.62	100	<0.02	<0.06	<0.002	<0.06	0.018
MW-2S	355428080493001	11-28-06	1.06	<0.1	7.6	0.24	12	<0.02	<0.06	<0.002	<0.06	<0.006
		07-10-07	1.23	<0.1	7.58	0.18	11	<0.02	<0.06	<0.002	<0.06	E 0.004
MW-2I	355428080493002	11-28-06	1.2	0.14	18.6	9.11	89	E 0.014	<0.06	<0.002	E 0.04	0.016
		07-10-07	1.31	0.1	21	8.79	88	<0.02	<0.06	<0.002	E 0.06	0.018
MW-2D	355428080493003	11-28-06	1.15	E 0.06	26.1	7.5	95	<0.02	<0.06	<0.002	<0.06	0.007
		07-09-07	1.12	E 0.07	25.6	7.45	97	<0.02	<0.06	<0.002	<0.06	0.008
MW-3S	355422080493101	11-29-06	4.2	<0.1	13.3	0.36	35	<0.02	0.22	<0.002	0.23	E 0.004
		07-11-07	4.03	<0.1	13.2	0.5	39	<0.02	0.53	<0.002	0.55	E 0.004
MW-3I	355422080493102	11-29-06	3.47	<0.1	22.1	1.4	65	<0.02	2.03	<0.002	2.12	0.011
		07-11-07	3.27	E 0.06	22.2	1.33	76	<0.02	2.18	<0.002	2.24	0.01
MW-3D	355422080493103	11-29-06	*	*	*	*	*	<0.02	<0.06	<0.002	<0.06	0.006
		07-10-07	*	*	*	*	*	<0.02	<0.06	<0.002	<0.06	0.009
MW-4S	355427080493701	11-29-06	1.37	<0.1	9.63	E 0.13	20	<0.02	<0.06	<0.002	<0.06	<0.006
		07-10-07	1.38	<0.1	9.3	<0.18	17	<0.02	<0.06	<0.002	<0.06	E 0.004
MW-4I	355427080493702	11-29-06	1.19	<0.1	23.8	1.65	59	<0.02	<0.06	<0.002	<0.06	0.025
		07-10-07	1.21	<0.1	24	1.51	51	<0.02	<0.06	<0.002	<0.06	0.027
MW-4D	355427080493703	11-29-06	*	*	*	*	*	<0.02	<0.06	E 0.001	<0.06	E 0.006
		07-10-07	*	*	*	*	*	<0.02	<0.06	0.006	<0.06	0.007
STREAM	02117495	07-11-07	2.58	<0.1	16.7	0.95	49	0.022	0.71	E 0.001	0.77	0.006

* Not analyzed or not reported due to suspected grout contamination.

Appendix 2. Analytical water-quality results from samples collected in November 2006 and July 2007 at the Allison Woods research station, Iredell County, North Carolina.—Continued

[mg/L, milligrams per liter; μS/cm, microsiemens per centimeter at 25 degrees Celsius; C, degrees Celsius; CaCO₃, calcium carbonate; E, estimated; <, less than; μg/L, micrograms per liter; N, Nitrogen]

Well number	Station number	Sample date	Aluminum, dissolved (μg/L)	Antimony, dissolved (μg/L)	Arsenic, dissolved (μg/L)	Barium, dissolved (μg/L)	Beryllium, dissolved (μg/L)	Boron, dissolved (μg/L)	Cadmium, dissolved (μg/L)	Chromium, dissolved (μg/L)	Cobalt, dissolved (μg/L)	Copper, dissolved (μg/L)
MW-1I	3554290804922302	11-28-06	46	< 0.06	< 0.12	85	< 0.06	3.8	0.04	0.34	3.1	E 0.36
		07-09-07	3.4	< 0.06	< 0.12	63	< 0.06	2.5	E 0.03	0.38	1.3	E 0.39
MW-1D	3554290804922303	11-28-06	*	*	*	*	*	*	*	*	*	*
		07-09-07	*	*	*	*	*	*	*	*	*	*
CH-1	3554290804922304	11-28-06	3.8	0.06	< 0.12	67	< 0.06	2.9	< 0.04	0.69	0.16	< 0.4
MW-2S	3554280804930001	11-28-06	7.5	< 0.06	< 0.12	33	0.1	2.2	E 0.02	E 0.1	0.66	< 0.4
		07-10-07	6.5	< 0.06	< 0.12	33	0.12	E 1.5	E 0.02	E 0.11	0.26	E 0.34
MW-2I	3554280804930002	11-28-06	1.7	E 0.05	< 0.12	52	< 0.06	3.5	0.22	0.27	0.43	< 0.4
		07-10-07	4.1	E 0.03	< 0.12	56	< 0.06	13	0.19	0.23	0.41	E 0.25
MW-2D	3554280804930003	11-28-06	3	< 0.06	E 0.11	83	< 0.06	2.5	< 0.04	0.17	0.15	< 0.4
		07-09-07	3	E 0.03	E 0.09	83	< 0.06	3.5	< 0.04	0.27	0.54	E 0.29
MW-3S	3554220804931101	11-29-06	4.1	< 0.06	< 0.12	41	0.1	3	< 0.04	0.51	0.32	0.71
		07-11-07	5.3	< 0.06	< 0.12	41	0.09	E 1.7	< 0.04	0.54	0.15	< 0.4
MW-3I	3554220804931102	11-29-06	< 1.6	< 0.06	< 0.12	87	< 0.06	1.9	< 0.04	0.29	0.2	E 0.28
		07-11-07	< 1.6	< 0.06	< 0.12	71	< 0.06	E 0.9	< 0.04	0.26	< 0.04	< 0.4
MW-3D	3554220804931103	11-29-06	*	*	*	*	*	*	*	*	*	*
		07-10-07	*	*	*	*	*	*	*	*	*	*
MW-4S	3554270804937701	11-29-06	1.6	< 0.06	< 0.12	16	0.08	2.6	< 0.04	0.87	0.11	< 0.4
		07-10-07	2	< 0.06	< 0.12	16	0.08	E 1.2	< 0.04	0.91	0.09	0.6
MW-4I	3554270804937702	11-29-06	< 1.6	< 0.06	< 0.12	23	< 0.06	2.9	< 0.04	0.6	E 0.03	< 0.4
		07-10-07	< 1.6	< 0.06	< 0.12	22	< 0.06	2	< 0.04	0.71	0.04	< 0.4
MW-4D	3554270804937703	11-29-06	*	*	*	*	*	*	*	*	*	*
		07-10-07	*	*	*	*	*	*	*	*	*	*
STREAM	02117495	07-11-07	15.7	< 0.06	< 0.12	35	< 0.06	E 1.2	< 0.04	0.34	0.33	< 0.4

* Not analyzed or not reported due to suspected grout contamination.

Appendix 2. Analytical water-quality results from samples collected in November 2006 and July 2007 at the Allison Woods research station, Iredell County, North Carolina.—Continued

[mg/L, milligrams per liter; µS/cm, microsiemens per centimeter at 25 degrees Celsius; C, degrees Celsius; CaCO₃, calcium carbonate; E, estimated; <, less than; µg/L, micrograms per liter; N, Nitrogen]

Well number	Station number	Sample date	Iron, dissolved (µg/L)	Lead, dissolved (µg/L)	Manganese, dissolved (µg/L)	Molybdenum, dissolved (µg/L)	Nickel, dissolved (µg/L)	Selenium, dissolved (µg/L)	Silver, dissolved (µg/L)	Zinc, dissolved (µg/L)	Radon-222 2-sigma combined uncertainty, water, unfiltered, picocuries per liter	Radon-222, water, unfiltered, picocuries per liter
MW-11	355429080492302	11-28-06	E 3	0.26	177	0.5	4.5	0.32	<0.1	10	*	*
		07-09-07	<6	<0.12	88.1	0.4	3	0.22	<0.1	5.1	24	470
MW-1D	355429080492303	11-28-06	*	*	*	*	*	*	*	*	*	*
		07-09-07	*	*	*	*	*	*	*	*	36	1430
CH-1	355429080492304	11-28-06	7	<0.12	27.3	1	1.2	0.17	<0.1	1.4	*	*
MW-2S	355428080493001	11-28-06	<6	<0.12	19.8	<0.1	0.47	<0.08	<0.1	7.2	*	*
		07-10-07	<6	0.4	11	<0.1	0.44	<0.08	<0.1	8.5	38	1530
MW-2I	355428080493002	11-28-06	<6	0.25	139	0.6	0.77	0.13	<0.1	9.3	*	*
		07-10-07	<6	E 0.1	150	0.4	0.61	0.08	<0.1	21	25	950
MW-2D	355428080493003	11-28-06	27	0.31	10.1	0.6	2	0.27	<0.1	66	*	*
		07-09-07	14	0.36	9.5	0.5	4.5	0.28	<0.1	49	49	2880
MW-3S	355422080493101	11-29-06	<6	0.12	18.7	<0.1	0.65	<0.08	<0.1	5.6	*	*
		07-11-07	<6	E 0.11	13.8	<0.1	0.63	<0.08	<0.1	2.3	28	800
MW-3I	355422080493102	11-29-06	<6	E 0.06	53.7	<0.1	1.7	E 0.04	<0.1	2.6	*	*
		07-11-07	<6	<0.12	22.1	<0.1	1.5	<0.08	<0.1	1.5	29	940
MW-3D	355422080493103	11-29-06	*	*	*	*	*	*	*	*	*	*
		07-10-07	*	*	*	*	*	*	*	*	30	950
MW-4S	355427080493701	11-29-06	<6	<0.12	4.4	<0.1	0.51	<0.08	<0.1	2.8	*	*
		07-10-07	<6	0.2	3.7	<0.1	0.51	<0.08	<0.1	2.9	31	990
MW-4I	355427080493702	11-29-06	<6	<0.12	0.9	E 0.1	0.27	E 0.06	<0.1	0.6	*	*
		07-10-07	<6	<0.12	0.8	E 0.1	0.32	E 0.05	<0.1	<0.6	37	1540
MW-4D	355427080493703	11-29-06	*	*	*	*	*	*	*	*	*	*
		07-10-07	*	*	*	*	*	*	*	*	32	1090
STREAM	02117495	07-11-07	69	<0.12	99.8	<0.1	0.24	<0.08	<0.1	0.8	*	*

* Not analyzed or not reported due to suspected grout contamination.